# *The* POWER *to* PROSPER

## KAP CHATFIELD

**CHARISMA HOUSE**

Used by permission of Tyndale House Publishers, Carol Stream, Illinois 60188. All rights reserved.

While the author has made every effort to provide accurate, up-to-date source information at the time of publication, statistics and other data are constantly updated. Neither the publisher nor the author assumes any responsibility for errors or for changes that occur after publication. Further, the publisher and author do not have any control over and do not assume any responsibility for third-party websites or their content.

For more resources like this, visit MyCharismaShop.com and the author's website at kapchatfield.com.

Cataloging-in-Publication Data is on file with the Library of Congress.
International Standard Book Number: 978-1-63641-534-5
E-book ISBN: 978-1-63641-535-2

1 2025
Printed in the United States of America

Most Charisma Media products are available at special quantity discounts for bulk purchase for sales promotions, premiums, fund-raising, and educational needs. For details, call us at (407) 333-0600 or visit our website at charismamedia.com.

*And you shall remember the LORD your God, for it is He who gives you power to get wealth, that He may establish His covenant which He swore to your fathers, as it is this day.*
—DEUTERONOMY 8:18

# CONTENTS

## Part IV: The Purpose of Prosperity

# FOREWORD

I'VE HAD THE honor and privilege to walk alongside Kap for over a decade now and am blessed to call him one of my best friends on this planet. God has gifted Kap with an electric personality and a five-talent gift set. He doesn't just preach the truth; he also practices it. I love how he loves his wife and children and leads in the local church.

When he walks into an environment, the room immediately changes as a result of the power of God through Him. It's a joyful, energetic, and prophetic presence. He has also stewarded His phenomenal gift set with such diligence that God has multiplied it to bless millions of us who have the privilege of being his friends.

In his book *The Power to Prosper*, you will glean biblical, practical, and powerful clarity on what true prosperity is all about. As a lead pastor for over seventeen years, my heart has hurt that so many of us have never truly understood what biblical prosperity, generosity, and stewardship is all about. Kap does such a phenomenal job of sharing Spirit-led clarity, biblical accuracy, and personal stories to equip and engage us all on this often misunderstood topic.

I am excited to see how God uses this work to bless so many as we continue on our journey of God-honoring stewardship and remove the lid that many of us place on ourselves, our families, our churches, and our businesses. This will be a classic handbook to help many churches learn what the Scriptures teach about true prosperity. We are no longer throwing the baby out with the bathwater when it comes to prosperity. We are leaning in to learn from someone who broke through the lies and can help us do the same!

My challenge to you is to set aside some unhurried, undistracted time to pray and ask God to guide you through this powerful and practical book. Let the Spirit of God clear up some questions you have and maybe even correct some long-held beliefs that don't align with God's best for your life.

With love and respect,

—PASTOR TODD DOXZON
FOUNDING AND LEAD PASTOR, LOVE CHURCH
OMAHA, NEBRASKA

# THE BOOK I WAS AFRAID TO WRITE

THIS IS THE book I didn't want to write. Not because I didn't believe it or wasn't living it but because I knew what it would cost. The moment I started talking about biblical prosperity, I would be misunderstood—labeled, judged, written off, maybe even mocked. People would inevitably lump me in with every manipulative preacher they've seen on late-night Christian TV.

The backlash would come from both the world and the church itself. I'd be accused of selling out, of chasing money, of watering down the gospel for worldly gain. No matter how many scriptures I quoted, how carefully I explained my heart, or how faithfully I lived my life, many would dismiss me because the word *prosperity* has already been poisoned.

Honestly, I understand why. We've all witnessed the abuses, cringed at the emotional manipulation, and heard hollow promises that had more to do with greed than God. But just because some people have abused prosperity doesn't mean we throw out God's promises altogether. Just because some preachers twisted it for personal gain doesn't mean we forget what the Bible actually says.

The deeper I went into the Word, the more I realized God never changed His mind about blessing His people. What He promised Abraham wasn't just for Abraham; it was for his descendants. Scripture affirms that if we belong to Christ, then we are Abraham's seed and heirs according to the promise (Gal. 3:29). Those who rightly divide the Word do not need to be ashamed (2 Tim. 2:15).

I couldn't deny what God had done in my own life. There was a time when I was following Jesus faithfully, preaching the gospel, creating content, building ministry, yet still panicking about money behind the scenes. I had surrendered my business and walked away from my main source of income. I had said yes to the call of full-time ministry, but the fear of financial failure hung over me like a cloud.

I couldn't afford a baseball helmet and bat for my son. I prayed desperately through Joy's medical bills and questioned why obedience had seemingly led me into lack. It was in that place, when I had no backup plan left, that God confronted my unbelief. He showed me that I trusted Him for salvation but not for provision. I preached the kingdom but lived like an orphan, waiting for a breakthrough while refusing to work the biblical principles He had already laid out for me to walk in.

God hadn't failed to provide; I had failed to believe what He actually promised. He had made a way, but I was too afraid to step into it. Once I saw it, I couldn't unsee it. Once I tasted the goodness of God's covenant—the full covenant—I couldn't go back.

What I've seen happening in the church today breaks my heart. We have a generation of sincere, Bible-believing Christians who love God but are financially broke, frustrated, and paralyzed by fear. They believe in salvation yet reject provision. They trust God for heaven while worrying about rent. They pray for breakthrough without ever expecting increase.

These believers have been taught that money is dangerous, that prosperity is prideful, that desire for more is somehow demonic. Meanwhile, people who deny God altogether are building companies, influencing culture, funding ideologies, and discipling nations with their wealth.

The church is begging. The world is prospering.

I had to ask myself: What if the prosperity problem in the church isn't because we've believed too much but because we've believed too little? What if we've let fear, religion, and bad theology keep us from walking in what Jesus paid for? What if we've been afraid to embrace the very promise that would set us free—not just spiritually but economically, socially, and generationally? What if God actually wants us to prosper so we can accomplish His purpose on the earth?

That's what this book is about. I'm not writing this to defend ministers who preach prosperity unbiblically or to make you selfishly rich at the expense of your eternal inheritance. I'm writing this book because I believe the church has forgotten something essential: Our God is a covenant-making, promise-keeping Father, and part of that covenant includes prosperity.

This is also not a book to bash people or ministers with nice things. For the record, I'm not against wearing nice clothes, living in nice houses, taking nice vacations, and so forth. Having nice things isn't the problem, but nice things *having you* is.

In this book I want to make the case that biblical prosperity is about having more than enough to take care of you, your family, and the people close to you while fulfilling assignments and creating generational impact. It's ultimately about funding missions, building churches, creating jobs, lifting communities, discipling nations. This is about the kingdom of God advancing through sons and daughters who are fully resourced to fulfill their callings.

We are living in prophetic days. Global systems are shifting, culture is spiraling, and the church can no longer afford to be broke and bashful about money. We are either going to rise in our God-given power to create wealth, or we're going to bow to the world's economy. There will be no neutral ground.

The Bible says in Deuteronomy 8:18:

> Remember the LORD your God, for it is He who gives you power to get wealth, that He may establish His covenant.

This verse is the framework for everything that follows. It's not a heretical slogan; it's covenant theology. It's a reminder that wealth isn't about greed but about mission, about establishing and demonstrating God's covenant on the earth.

In the chapters ahead I'm going to walk you through why the church has rejected prosperity and what it's cost us. I'm going to show you what God's covenant actually promises when it comes to wealth. I'm going to teach you how to discover and activate the power He's placed inside you to create value and help you learn how to steward prosperity without losing your soul.

I'll be honest with you up front: *Prosperity comes with persecution.* There's a reason most pastors won't touch this topic and why I hesitated to write about it. As soon as you start prospering God's way and teaching others how to do it, you become a target. You're misunderstood, criticized, and accused of greed even when your motives are pure.

Still, I'd rather be persecuted for obeying God than applauded for playing it safe.

Truthfully, I couldn't stay silent. Not after what I've seen. I've lost count of how many people have reached out to me, desperate for prayer over their finances. I've seen the tears, read the DMs, and heard the cries of people who love God but feel stuck in lack.

I've also seen what happens when they finally believe what God says about wealth and act on it. I've received countless testimonies from people who started applying the Word of God, and everything began to change.

Their income increased, their confidence grew, their faith deepened, and their impact multiplied.

That's why I had to write this. Because I know the fruit of this message and have watched it transform lives, including my own. I believe we're only beginning to understand how important this is, not just for today but for the days to come.

Here's something most pastors aren't talking about: What if our understanding of prosperity has more to do with end-time events than we realize? What if how we view money and provision is what determines who we trust when the systems of the world start to collapse? What if this conversation isn't just about financial increase but spiritual allegiance?

The world is waiting. The harvest is ready. And it's going to take more than prayers and sermons to reach them.

*It will take godly prosperity.*

# BEFORE YOU BEGIN

To help you apply what you're about to read, I've created a full library of resources, tools, and video content to help you walk out this message in real time. Throughout these pages, you'll find QR codes like the one below linking you to:

- video teachings that go deeper into each chapter
- bonus content and behind-the-scenes insight
- worksheets and exercises to apply the principles
- declarations and prayers for ongoing breakthrough
- access to the Power to Prosper online community

This message isn't just meant to be read; it's meant to be lived. I encourage you to access these additional resources by scanning the QR codes or visiting thepowertoprosperbook.com/resources.

# PART I

# THE PROBLEM AROUND PROSPERITY

## CHAPTER 1

# THE DAY EVERYTHING CHANGED

**M**EET ME AT the ER."

That text changed everything.

My wife, Joy, sent it after a routine workout turned into something we never expected. She had been feeling off, so she checked her blood sugar levels. The reading was north of 400. If you know anything about diabetes, you know that's when organs start shutting down. We rushed her to the ER, and within hours doctors delivered the news: Joy was a type 1 diabetic. She also had three or four other autoimmune disorders we had never known about.

Our whole world flipped upside down in a moment.

What made it even harder was our existing financial situation. We had been struggling for years while I tried to build a digital media company and serve in ministry simultaneously. I was doing everything possible to keep the business afloat: taking on debt to pay employees, hustling to keep clients happy, whatever it took. The truth was, we were barely scraping by.

We didn't even have health insurance. As a struggling entrepreneur, it was just one more thing we had put off, hoping we wouldn't need it. Now here we were with hospital bills piling up, savings draining fast, and no safety net to catch us.

The weight of feeling unable to provide had been crushing me for years. When my son wanted to play T-ball at three years old, I couldn't afford to buy him a bat, glove, or helmet. Embarrassed, I had to ask other dads whether we could borrow their kids' equipment. I felt like a total failure as a father. Watching *It's a Wonderful Life*, I'd see George Bailey breaking down because he couldn't provide for his family, and I would weep because that was exactly how I felt.

I used to watch the end of that movie thinking, "I wish my story would end like that. I wish it would all work out for me."

Now, facing this health crisis with Joy, already buried in business debt, with no backup plan in sight, I hit rock bottom.

I cried out to God in frustration and confusion. "God, what gives? I'm trying to honor You. I'm trying to build something good. Why is this happening?"

That's when He spoke.

"Kap, you've got Matthew 6:33 backward."

The verse says, "Seek *first* the kingdom of God and His righteousness, and all these things shall be added to you" (emphasis added).

But I wasn't seeking the kingdom first. I was seeking business, clients, provision, hoping the kingdom would somehow fit into the margins.

It broke me. It reset me.

I realized I had been trying to serve two masters without even knowing it. I had let the spirit of mammon creep into my thinking, the spirit that says, "Take care of yourself, trust in your hustle, build your own future." It wasn't just about chasing money; it was about the order of my heart.

God wasn't merely trying to fix our financial situation. He was after my foundation.

During that season, Joy looked at me through all the chaos and uncertainty and said, "I trust you. I trust Christ in you."

Those words wrecked me in the best way. I knew I couldn't play it safe anymore or stay stuck trying to make things happen through my own strength. God was inviting me to surrender fully, not just my ministry dreams but my provision, strategy, and future.

He asked me a question that changed everything: "Do you believe I'm a better Master than the world?"

That was the line in the sand. I had to choose, not just once, but daily. I had to surrender my business, my pride, my survival instincts, and my fear that following God fully would cause my family to suffer financially.

I said yes.

I gave God my yes with no backup plan. Four months of savings remained, enough to get us through if nothing else worked. I told Joy, "I'm going all in on creating content for the kingdom. I don't know how it will monetize or how God will provide. All I know is that this is what He's asking me to do."

For four months I showed up every single day. Three videos daily, with rare exceptions. Some days it was two videos. Some days I missed one. Mostly, it was three to four videos, no excuses, no backup plan, no Plan B.

Initially, it felt worse, not better. With each video posted, instead of gaining traction, I was losing followers. Every time I refreshed the page, it felt like another person had walked out. It wasn't just discouraging; it was humiliating. Here I was, finally stepping out in obedience, finally doing what God told me to do, yet by every visible metric it appeared to be failing.

I kept showing up anyway.

Then, unexpectedly, an Instagram video went viral. It wasn't the one I thought would succeed or had obsessed over trying to perfect. It was simply the fruit of obedience. One video turned into two. Two turned into ten. Momentum began building as Instagram caught fire, then TikTok, then Facebook. Platforms I hadn't even prioritized suddenly exploded with growth.

YouTube, the platform I was banking on most, remained stubbornly silent. For four months it felt like planting seeds in hard, dry ground with no visible results. Right at the end of that fourth month, YouTube finally broke open.

Before the breakthrough, I almost quit. About two months into the journey, someone made a viral video about me, calling me a false teacher. They twisted my words and mocked my ministry. Suddenly, my inbox, comment sections, and DMs flooded with criticism. Strangers worldwide told me to quit, called me a fraud, and accused me of deceiving people.

It crushed me.

Walking into church one Sunday, someone approached me saying, "Dude, are you OK? I just saw a thread about you on Reddit...they were trashing you." I was ready to give up. I wasn't even making money yet, still living off savings while trying to be obedient.

That weekend my family took a spontaneous road trip to Texas to clear our heads. Standing in the hotel shower, exhausted and defeated, I said to God, "This isn't working. I don't want to do this anymore."

He spoke to me again: "Let me ask you a question, Kap. If I snapped My fingers and filled your bank account with all the money you could ever ask for, would you be happy?"

I paused before answering, "No."

Deep down I knew it was true. No amount of money would fix what was broken inside.

"That's right," He continued. "Because if everything around you changed while *you* remained the same, it would all be meaningless. I need to prove to you that I've already placed the power to prosper within you."

It wasn't a resource problem. It was a resourcefulness problem. God wasn't trying to just fix our external situation. He was trying to draw out something He had already placed inside me.

Encouraged by this revelation, I made a decision: "God, nevertheless, at Your word, I'll let down my net." Like Peter, who fished all night catching nothing, I chose to obey when everything within me wanted to quit.

That's when everything changed.

People began finding salvation through the content. Messages poured in from around the world: "Your video led me to Jesus" or "God used your words to bring me back to Him." Though financial fruit hadn't appeared yet, the eternal fruit was growing visibly. That alone sustained me.

At the four-month mark, everything shifted. I went from 1,000 to 10,000 YouTube subscribers in four months, from 10,000 to 100,000 in twenty-eight days, from 100,000 to 200,000 in just ten more days. Within the year, I crossed a million subscribers.

It wasn't just YouTube. Opportunities I could never have orchestrated began appearing. Access to people I never could have reached before. Financial provision that transformed our family's life. Everything exploded, not because I chased it but because I chased Him.

Looking back now, the greatest miracle wasn't the platform, money, or opportunities. Through the struggle, pressure, and refining fire, I discovered who God truly is: Jehovah Jireh, the Lord who provides. He is the source, not just the supplier. He is the prosperer.

He wanted more than to just meet my needs; He wanted to form my faith. He wanted to prove He had placed supernatural power within me. It was the power to create wealth, generate value, and prosper. No system, critic, or demon could ever take that away.

This isn't about prosperity as theory or treating God like a genie. It's about fully allowing Him to build a testimony of abundance through us that shuts the door to the spirit of mammon in our lives once and for all.

If He did it for me, He can do it for you.

To access additional resources, scan the QR code or visit thepowertoprosperbook.com/resources.

## CHAPTER 2

# SATAN'S MOST DECEITFUL STRATEGY—KEEP THE CHURCH BROKE

**S**ATAN ISN'T JUST afraid of a praying church. He's afraid of a well-financed one. We've made revival all about feelings and fire tunnels, but when you look at the Book of Acts, revival wasn't just an emotional outpouring. It was followed by radical generosity, resource distribution, and infrastructure for sustainable impact.

The Bible says in Acts 4:32–35 that the believers were of one heart and one soul, and no one claimed that any of their possessions was their own, but they shared everything they had. With great power the apostles continued to testify to the resurrection of the Lord Jesus, and God's grace was so powerfully at work in them that there were no needy persons among them. Revival wasn't just a service but a system. Not just fire on the altar but stewardship in the community.

If I were the devil, and I couldn't stop people from getting saved, my strategy would be clear: Keep them broke, convince them poverty is holy, twist Scripture to make prosperity look evil, make ministers feel guilty for raising support, and cause entrepreneurs to feel worldly for wanting to grow. This strategy would keep God's people small so they couldn't fund big things. It would keep their dreams microscopic so that their impact stayed minimal. And honestly? It has worked.

For a long time this lie shaped my own beliefs. Money talk seemed likely to make people stumble. Desiring increase appeared to contradict contentment. Asking for help, launching offers, or building business alongside ministry felt somehow unspiritual. These fears kept me playing small and safe with modest dreams and lower expectations. What I called humility was actually fear and bondage. The Holy Spirit eventually confronted me with a revelation: *This mindset isn't humility but a demonic stronghold.*

The truth is, the devil doesn't care whether you love God. He just wants to make sure you stay dependent on Pharaoh for your provision. He doesn't need you to become a heretic, just to stay small, safe, and broke. A financially limited believer can't fund a move of God. An under-resourced church can't shape culture. A cash-strapped generation can't disciple nations, and Satan knows it.

Jesus didn't say you can't serve both God and the devil. He said you can't serve both God and mammon (Matt. 6:24). Mammon isn't money. It's a spirit that tries to attach itself to money. It's the belief that money is your source, your protector, your safety net. The devil doesn't mind you singing songs about freedom as long as you're still loyal to Pharaoh when it comes to your provision. He wants you dependent on credit cards, broken government systems, and employers who control your time and values. If he can't control you through sin, he'll control you through scarcity.

The church fears money because we've witnessed the abuses of fake healers and manipulative preachers distorting "prosperity." This led to overcorrection where we abandoned teaching stewardship, honoring generosity, and expecting increase. Instead, we spiritualized poverty, acting as though financial struggle was more righteous than having resources.

Scripture never praises poverty, though it values contentment, warns about greed, and commands generosity. Poverty is never described as a virtue. It is consistently linked to destruction, injustice, or disobedience. Proverbs 13:18 (ESV) declares, "Poverty and disgrace come to him who ignores instruction." Proverbs 10:15 (NASB) states, "The ruin of the poor is their poverty." Proverbs 13:22 (ESV) affirms, "A good man leaves an inheritance to his children's children."

God is not against money. He is against money having you. Until we break agreement with the lie that God wants us broke, we will continue to sabotage our own harvest.

Hell's most effective strategy against the church isn't outright heresy but subtle idolatry. It keeps believers stuck in survival mode, buried under bills and fear. As long as you're thinking about survival, you're not thinking about strategy. When you're worried about paying rent, you're not funding revival. Being stuck in survival blocks you from stepping fully into divine assignments.

The devil doesn't fear your Bible knowledge if you're too broke to act on it. He doesn't fear your prayers if you can't fund what God told you to build, or your worship if your hands are tied by debt. As long as he can keep you living paycheck to paycheck, he can keep you from taking territory.

That's why the fight for financial freedom is spiritual before it's practical. You can budget all day and hustle all year, but if you don't break agreement with the lie that God wants you broke, you'll keep sabotaging your own harvest.

The solution for a broke church extends beyond better money management, side hustles, or savings accounts. It requires revelation and mind renewal. You need to be set free from inner vows like "I'll never be rich," "I don't need much," "Money always corrupts," "I'm just not a business person." These lies don't make you humble. They make you ineffective. The kingdom can't afford that anymore.

A prosperous church is a dangerous church—one that can fund its own missions, reclaim buildings, eliminate student debt, outgive secular foundations, and disciple creators, business owners, and political leaders. That's the church hell is terrified of, and that's the church Jesus is building.

This message will be attacked. You'll be misunderstood. People will twist your words, but we're not backing down. We're not building personal kingdoms but God's kingdom. His kingdom is powered not by excuses but by faith, obedience, stewardship, and supernatural provision. It's time to expose the lie. It's time to evict the fear. The church was never designed to be broke; it was designed to break chains.

## The Data Doesn't Lie

We see this reality not just in Scripture but in statistics. A 2016 Pew Research Center study on household income by US religious group revealed something sobering: Groups with minimal biblical emphasis on the Holy Spirit's power showed the greatest financial prosperity. 44 percent of Jewish households earned $100,000 or more per year, and next were Hindus (36 percent), Episcopalians (35 percent), and Presbyterians (32 percent); these groups were followed by atheists and agnostics.

Near the bottom were Pentecostal, Charismatic, and Evangelical churches: Assemblies of God (10 percent), American Baptist churches (9 percent), Church of God in Christ (9 percent), and National Baptist Convention (9 percent).[1] These are precisely the groups professing belief in

God's power, the Spirit's fullness, and heaven's supernatural provision, yet experiencing the greatest financial limitation.

How can believers who proclaim revival, pray in tongues, minister healing, and preach miracles possess the least financial influence? Why do churches claiming supernatural authority still depend on secular banks, government grants, and fundraising gimmicks just to keep the lights on? This isn't just a practical problem. It's a theological one. Our lack is preaching a message, and it's not the gospel.

A powerless gospel doesn't just show up in dead churches. It shows up in broke ones. It shows up in ministries that can preach fire but can't fund vision. It shows up in denominations preserving spiritual traditions while abandoning covenant prosperity. If we don't wake up soon, another generation will emerge shouting "revival" on Sundays while struggling in survival mode throughout the week.

We cannot keep ignoring this. The numbers don't lie. We've allowed ourselves to be convinced that financial lack is normal and that scraping by is just part of serving God. Somehow "just enough" has become more holy than "more than enough." The Word says otherwise.

This data confirms what the enemy has known for years: When the church is broke, the kingdom stalls. That's why this chapter matters. That's why this book matters. This isn't just about income brackets but about influence. It's about inheritance. It's about whether we're ready to fund what God has called us to build. If we're not, someone else will.

## Why Pastors Are Burning Out

This problem affects not just individual believers but leadership as well. A 2021 Barna Group study found that 38 percent of US pastors had seriously considered leaving full-time ministry that year—not from lost faith but from overwhelming financial and emotional pressure.[2] The issue wasn't moral failure or theological compromise but exhaustion, as pastors navigated global chaos, political division, and personal crises while privately drowning under financial strain.

This challenge isn't new. A 2015 National Association of Evangelicals study discovered that 76 percent of pastors knew colleagues who had left ministry due to financial pressures. Three out of four pastors witnessed others departing because of money concerns. With 90 percent reporting some level of personal financial stress, a disturbing pattern emerges: We've built a ministry culture where sacrifice is expected, but sustainability is rare.[3]

Those responsible for shepherding the flock, equipping saints, and building the kingdom burn out trying to make ends meet. While some churches thrive with million-dollar budgets, thousands of faithful leaders are quietly asking God how they're supposed to keep going. They fundraise for survival rather than expansion. They lead Sunday worship while contemplating Monday's need for a second job. Yet we normalize this situation in humility's name.

Nothing about this reflects humility or nobility. Watching spiritual leaders collapse under pressures we should share represents not a financial issue but a spiritual one. We've allowed a spirit of mammon to convince us that needing money is shameful, and that prospering in ministry is somehow selfish.

The Bible is clear: The laborer is worthy of his wages. Those who preach the gospel should live from the gospel. Those who lead well, especially in teaching and doctrine, are worthy of double honor. God doesn't expect pastors to live in poverty. He expects the church to provide for them so they can devote themselves fully to the Word and prayer.

We're losing not only current pastors but future church planters. In 2010 half of all surveyed church planters cited financial challenges as one of their biggest obstacles.[4] Many struggled to secure space, equipment, and basic tools for ministry. More recent research confirms that funding isn't just helpful but decisive. *Christianity Today* reported in 2023 that church plants with higher initial funding experienced significantly more growth. The attendance difference among churches launching with over 200 members versus under 100 often came down to about $100,000 in start-up and first-year investment.[5]

This topic isn't discussed enough in spiritual circles. Sometimes it's not a lack of vision that keeps churches small but a lack of funding. It's not always disobedience that shuts down a ministry—sometimes it's just financial suffocation. We've created a system where the most Spirit-filled leaders remain the least financially equipped, with devastating results: stunted church growth, pastoral burnout, and kingdom expansion bottlenecked by lack.

If we want to see revival, we need to stop romanticizing lack. Reaching cities, planting churches, and making disciples requires overcoming prosperity fears. What we're seeing isn't just a money problem but a resourcing problem. Without the church addressing this conversation with boldness, conviction, and biblical clarity, we'll continue watching effective leaders disappear and promising churches fail to establish roots.

To access additional resources, scan the QR code or visit thepowertoprosperbook. com/resources.

## CHAPTER 3

# PROSPERITY IS NOT A CURSE WORD

I F YOU GREW up in church like I did, you've probably heard some version of this: "Be careful with money; it's dangerous." "It's easier for a camel to go through the eye of a needle than for a rich man to enter heaven." "Jesus was poor, so you should be too." Then there's the ultimate stain on a preacher's reputation: being labeled a "prosperity gospel" preacher. For many, that title alone cancels out everything else a person says.

But here's where I've always found myself confused: If *prosperity* is such a bad word, then why does God say it so much throughout the Bible?

I mean, if prosperity were as spiritually toxic as we've been led to believe, God would have a lot of repenting to do. The word is all over Scripture. From Genesis to Revelation, prosperity isn't just mentioned, it's modeled. Abraham was blessed. Isaac was blessed. Jacob, Joseph, David, and Solomon were all blessed. Entire nations were blessed because of the covenant God had with His people.

So how did we get here? How did we become so afraid of a word that God clearly isn't afraid of?

Let me be clear: I'm not here to defend the prosperity gospel, however you want to define it. I'm not here to justify the abuses, the manipulation, the greed, or the seed-offering scams. Trust me, I've seen the clips and heard the stories. I've walked with people who were burned by the lie that you can buy a miracle from God if you just "sow a significant seed." I hate that distortion.

What I refuse to do is let the enemy twist a promise of God into something the church becomes ashamed of. While we can criticize the prosperity gospel, we cannot deny the prosperity *of* the gospel.

In my ten years of ministry, I've learned something about how the enemy operates. Satan doesn't create anything. Jesus referred to him as the thief who comes only to steal, kill, and destroy. That's exactly what he does: He counterfeits and perverts. The things he goes after the hardest tend to be the most valuable in the kingdom of God. Unfortunately, whenever he touches something, Christians want to throw the whole thing away.

Think about it. The church rejected deliverance ministry because some people made it weird. We rejected speaking in tongues because some operated in it without order, and others falsely taught that if you don't speak in tongues, you're not even saved. We rejected the prophetic because some words proved inaccurate or plain wrong. In each case, we overcorrected, silenced the Spirit to maintain safe services, and threw out the gift to avoid the abuse.

With prosperity, we did the same thing. We let the enemy rob us of a covenant promise. We forgot that it was God, not culture, who created the concept of blessing. We forgot that it was God who made Abraham rich, God who gave Joseph a divine strategy for economic survival, God who filled Solomon with wisdom and wealth, and God who "gives you power to get wealth" (Deut. 8:18). Prosperity didn't originate in a TV preacher's green room. It originated in the heart of a Father who loves to take care of His kids.

Because of a few misused verses and a lot of misbehaving preachers, we've made *prosperity* a curse word in the church. We whisper it like it's taboo. We distance ourselves from it so we don't look greedy. We spiritualize poverty and call it humility. As a result, we've created an entire generation of believers who love Jesus but live powerless, broke, and dependent on the very world system God called them to rise above.

That's not holiness. That's bondage.

Let's clarify something theologically: God doesn't want us enslaved to Egypt while calling it contentment. He never called His people to beg Pharaoh for provision. He called them to walk in covenant.

This is where it gets personal for me. For years I wrestled with this tension. I felt guilty for wanting more. I wondered whether it was wrong to build a business, make money, or dream bigger. I didn't want to be "that guy"—flashy, self-promoting, obsessed with materialism.

I couldn't shake the question: If God owns everything, why are His people living like beggars?

I remember creating videos and content and wondering whether I should even mention anything about giving, finances, or tithing. I'd post a clip about faith and get cheers. I'd post something about God wanting to bless people financially, and suddenly, the comments would erupt into a war zone. It seemed as though people were literally manifesting demons just because I said the word *prosperity* while quoting Scripture!

Here's the irony: The same people who criticize prosperity theology often message me privately to ask for prayer over their finances. So which is it? Does God care about our financial well-being or not? Is He a good Father or a distant one? Does He want us to have what we need to fulfill our assignment, or must we figure it out on our own?

I've learned that most people don't reject prosperity because of Scripture. They reject it because of bad, man-made doctrine. They saw some preachers abuse the promises of God (knowingly or unknowingly), and instead of getting clarity, they reacted emotionally. They clung to the phrase "prosperity gospel is heresy," recoiling every time the word *prosperity* was mentioned. They overcorrected, embraced struggle, and treated poverty as a badge of honor. In doing so, they surrendered territory God never told them to give up.

Let me be clear. This book is not about chasing money. This book is about money chasing you as you chase God's assignment for your life.

Prosperity—God's prosperity—means thriving in every area of life. Yes, it includes money, but money is the fruit on the tree, not the root that produces it. God's definition of prosperity isn't necessarily having a yacht and a Rolex. There's nothing wrong with those things, but that's not the point. The point is having more than enough to do everything God's called you to do, with enough left over to bless everyone connected to you.

God has no problem lavishing His kids with material blessings. In fact, I'd argue that kingdom prosperity should almost feel embarrassing because we don't deserve it. Jesus' first miracle was turning water into wine, and it wasn't a miracle of utility. It was a miracle of luxury.

That's the kind of Father we serve: not insecure about blessing His children, not worried about looking greedy, not ashamed of giving good gifts. He's a good Father, and good fathers rejoice when their kids flourish, not when they're broke.

We're going to reclaim the word *prosperity*. Not for greed's sake but for covenant's sake. It's time to stop apologizing for wanting to build, grow, lead, multiply, create, give, and fund the end-time revival. It's time to stop confusing poverty with piety and remember that God is a good Father who wants His kids walking in abundance, with open hands and full hearts, ready to bless everyone around them.

So let's say it boldly and without shame: Prosperity is not a curse word. It's a promise from God.

If we're going to reclaim prosperity, we must first clear the rubble and uproot the lies that have choked the church for too long. We must expose every false belief that's kept God's people broke, fearful, and spiritually paralyzed. You can't walk in a promise you're still suspicious of, and you can't steward what you secretly resent. So before we move forward, let's take a hard look at the lies and replace them with the truth.

## Lie #1: Money buys miracles.

This is probably one of the most damaging distortions in Charismatic circles. Somewhere along the way people were led to believe that if you just "sow a seed," you can force God's hand and that if you give a certain amount, He owes you a breakthrough, particularly in the areas of healing and deliverance. I know a person who was duped into believing that if she sowed her entire inheritance, God would heal her mother of multiple sclerosis. She sowed the inheritance, and her mother's healing never manifested.

Whoever taught her that wasn't teaching faith; they were either ignorantly teaching heresy or outright manipulating her. God doesn't respond to bribes; He responds to faith. You can't buy a miracle, and anyone who told you otherwise lied to you.

Yes, giving is biblical, and yes, generosity unlocks blessing. Sowing and reaping financially is a biblical principle I'll touch on later in this book, but a seed only bears fruit of its own kind. In the same way you can't sow an apple seed and expect an orange tree to come out of the ground, you can't give to God financially and expect to reap a miracle. There's no biblical precedent for that.

When we give to God with a cheerful heart, He does bless us, but His blessing isn't transactional; it's relational.

## Lie #2: God never blesses materially.

I'm not sure what Bible people are reading when they say this, but it's not the one I'm holding. From Genesis to Revelation, God's covenant with His people consistently includes material blessing. Abraham was made "very rich in livestock, in silver, and in gold" (Gen. 13:2). Isaac sowed in famine and reaped a hundredfold, and Solomon was the wealthiest king of his time, with wealth coming directly from the wisdom God gave him. The early church shared resources so powerfully that "there was not a needy person among them" (Acts 4:34, ESV), and even in eternity the streets are paved with gold.

God is not allergic to wealth; nor is He anti-abundance. What He opposes is people trusting in riches instead of trusting in Him. Let's not pretend that material blessing is off-limits in the kingdom, as it remains part of the covenant.

## Lie #3: Money is evil.

This is one of the most misquoted verses in the entire Bible and an all-time classic lie. Scripture doesn't say that money is the root of all evil. It says, "The *love* of money is a root of all kinds of evil" (1 Tim. 6:10, emphasis added). That's a huge difference.

Money is neutral; it's a tool that takes on the character of the person using it. A wicked person uses money to exploit others. A righteous person uses money to build hospitals, plant churches, rescue orphans, and feed the hungry. God created gold and called it good, and designed Eden with resources embedded in the soil. Jesus Himself said we should use "unrighteous mammon" to make an eternal impact and win friends for eternity (Luke 16:9).

If money were evil, Jesus wouldn't have taught so much about it, God wouldn't give us instructions on how to steward it, and the church would have no business asking for it. The truth is, money in the hands of a righteous person can fund the gospel, break chains, and advance the kingdom. The issue isn't the money; it's whether the money has you. Money is not evil; it's essential!

## Lie #4: Prosperity is just an American idea.

This one makes me laugh. As if Abraham, Isaac, Jacob, Joseph, David, Solomon, and Jesus Himself were all raised in the American Dream. The idea that prosperity is a Western or capitalist construct is not only ignorant but unbiblical. Prosperity didn't start in Dallas or Los Angeles; it started in Eden. The garden was filled with gold, fruit-bearing trees, and rivers that nourished the land.

Throughout Scripture we see God prospering people from the Middle East, Africa, and Asia long before America was ever a nation. This promise was never limited by geography; it was always about covenant.

## Lie #5: The church just wants your money.

Let's be honest: Sometimes this one is true. There are ministries that have mishandled finances and churches that have guilted people into giving while

17

lacking accountability and transparency. Some leaders have manipulated people emotionally for financial gain, and that's wrong. However, just because some have misused funds doesn't mean the entire church is corrupt, nor does it mean you should withhold your tithe and offerings out of bitterness.

The church doesn't need your money because it's desperate. God doesn't want your money because He needs it; He owns the cattle on a thousand hills. The church invites your giving because giving is how God matures you, how you break agreement with the spirit of mammon, and how you partner with the mission of heaven. When the church teaches on finances with biblical clarity and kingdom purpose, it's not about extracting from people but equipping them to live in covenant blessing.

Jesus talked more about money than heaven and hell combined because He knew that where your treasure is, your heart is also. God wants your money because He wants your heart. Teaching people to tithe, to be generous, and to trust God with their finances isn't manipulation; it's good shepherding.

The church isn't trying to take something from you; it's trying to help unlock something *for* you. A healthy church doesn't just take offerings. It teaches people how to walk in financial freedom so they can fund their assignment and live a life of generosity without fear.

## Lie #6: God promises persecution, not prosperity.

This one always fascinates me, as if persecution and prosperity are mutually exclusive. The truth is, they often go hand in hand. Jesus promised persecution, yes. But He also promised that those who give up everything for His sake will receive a hundredfold *"in the present age"* with persecution and eternal life in the age to come (Mark 10:29–30, NASB, emphasis added). Paul was persecuted, but he also said, "My God shall supply all your need according to His riches in glory" (Phil. 4:19).

You can be blessed and still be battle-tested; you can be resourced and still rejected. Prosperity doesn't cancel out persecution. In fact, it often provokes it, but both are part of the promise.

## Lie #7: Poverty brings out the best in people.

There's a popular idea in church culture that poverty makes people humble, that it strips away distractions and draws you closer to God. While there's no doubt that suffering can refine someone's faith, let's not confuse refinement with God's original intent. Poverty doesn't make people holy; it makes people desperate. It pushes families into cycles of dysfunction and increases the risk of addiction, anxiety, crime, abuse, and depression. There's a reason Proverbs says, "The ruin of the poor is their poverty" (10:15, AMP). That's not a poetic metaphor. It's reality.

Yes, God meets us in the valley, and yes, He can use trials to produce perseverance. But that doesn't mean poverty is His design. God's design is for people to thrive spiritually, emotionally, and materially so they can be a blessing to others. When the church romanticizes struggle and glorifies lack, we're not honoring God. We're misrepresenting Him.

## Lie #8: Rich people are spoiled.

There's a quiet resentment in Christian circles toward wealth. Even among believers, there's often an unspoken suspicion that if someone is wealthy, they must be selfish, prideful, or disconnected from "real" spiritual life. But that's not a biblical assumption. Abraham was wealthy, and he was called a friend of God. David was wealthy, and he was a man after God's own heart. Job, Solomon, Joseph, Boaz, Lydia—wealth was part of their testimony, not a threat to it.

Spoiled people aren't produced by money. They're produced by entitlement and poor character. Having money doesn't corrupt someone. It exposes what's already in them. In the hands of a righteous person, wealth becomes a weapon for good that can rescue families, plant churches, disciple cities, and transform nations. If anything, it's time for more godly people to become wealthy so the world can see what wealth is supposed to look like when it's submitted to the King.

## Lie #9: God hates prosperity.

This one might be the most ironic because from Genesis to Revelation the Bible reveals a God who delights in blessing His people. He placed Adam and Eve in a garden filled with gold, fruit, and beauty, and He called it "very good." When He gave the Israelites the Promised Land, it was described as flowing with milk and honey. The kingdom of heaven is paved with streets of gold. The new heaven and new earth is a place with no pain, no tears, no death, and certainly no poverty. When Jesus walked the earth, He alleviated suffering, restored dignity, and brought supernatural provision wherever He went.

You cannot reconcile a God who calls prosperity "good" with the idea that He's against your increase. He's not offended by abundance. He invented it. If heaven is His standard, why would we treat prosperity like it's unholy? Why would we call evil what God called good?

## Lie #10: I need to chase money to have more of it.

This lie is subtle because it appeals to our flesh while sounding responsible. Culture teaches us that if we want to get ahead, we have to chase the bag, hustle harder, work longer, and stack the next check. But Jesus didn't teach that. Jesus said to seek first the kingdom of God and His righteousness, and all these "things," including financial provision, would be added unto you (Matt. 6:33). You don't chase money. You chase God, and money follows obedience.

I think about my friends Kevin and Bree. When they restructured their ministry, they made one simple shift: They started measuring success by how much time they spent in prayer, not by metrics or money. Within months, their ministry saw rapid growth through new partnerships, financial breakthroughs, and supernatural provision, all following their renewed focus. They didn't chase money. They chased God, and as a result, money chased them.

## Lie #11: When somebody is rich, somebody else has to be poor.

This is the scarcity mindset at its root. It assumes that the economic pie is fixed, so if one person has a larger slice, someone else must go hungry. However, that's not how the kingdom works. God is not limited by zero-sum thinking, as He's a Creator and Jesus is a multiplier. God doesn't divide scarcity. He multiplies supply.

Think about Elisha and the widow in 2 Kings 4. She was on the brink of losing her sons to slavery with only a small jar of oil left. Elisha gave her one instruction: Gather empty vessels. As she obeyed, the oil kept flowing, stopping only when there were no more containers. The problem wasn't God's supply but her capacity. In the kingdom, there's always more where that came from.

## Lie #12: God's financial promises were only for the spiritual forefathers.

Some say that all the blessings in the Old Testament—Abraham's wealth, Isaac's harvest, Joseph's elevation—were only for that generation, but Galatians 3 destroys that argument. Paul writes that if you belong to Christ, you are Abraham's seed and heirs according to the promise, meaning everything God promised Abraham is now available to you through faith.

This isn't about being Jewish by blood but about being grafted in by covenant. The promises weren't revoked when Jesus came; they were fulfilled. Now, through Christ, we have access to every spiritual and material blessing connected to the covenant. You don't have to earn it. You inherit it.

## Lie #13: Wealth will make you hate God.

One of the most toxic lies Christians have believed is that material blessing will automatically lead you away from God and that the moment you prosper you'll forget where you came from and abandon your faith. Scripture shows otherwise. When Peter experienced one of the greatest business blessings of his life—when Jesus told him to cast his nets again, and he pulled in so much fish that his boat began to sink—what did Peter do? He didn't curse God, get cocky, or leave the faith. Instead, he fell to his knees and worshipped. The blessing didn't push him away but pulled him closer.

Prosperity in the right heart doesn't breed pride. It stirs praise. The problem isn't wealth; it's forgetting where it came from. Peter didn't forget.

## Lie #14: Nobody holy in the Bible was rich.

This lie collapses the moment you actually open your Bible. Abraham was rich, Isaac was rich, and Jacob was rich. Joseph became second-in-command over the wealth of Egypt, while Job was the wealthiest man in the East before and after his trial. David was wealthy enough to fund the building of the temple, and Solomon was so wealthy and wise that kings and queens traveled across continents just to sit in his presence. Boaz was a wealthy landowner, while Esther lived in royal luxury and leveraged her position to save her people.

Wealth wasn't a rare exception among the righteous. It was often a sign of God's covenant blessing at work in their lives.

## Lie #15: Prosperity is random.

Some people talk about prosperity as if it's a spiritual lottery, completely random and out of your control. But Scripture tells a different story. Prosperity isn't a matter of chance; it's shaped by principles. You receive what you believe and what you speak, and you reap what you sow. If you're diligent, you'll increase; but if you're lazy, you won't. Greed brings sorrow. Dishonoring your marriage drains your wealth. Withholding your tithe closes the windows of heaven over your life.

Prosperity isn't about luck. It's the fruit of covenant alignment and consistent obedience.

## Lie #16: Poverty equals holiness.

This is one of the deadliest lies because it sounds so spiritual. It paints struggle as sacred and lack as a badge of honor. But poverty in and of itself doesn't make anyone holy. In fact, Scripture says poverty ruins lives and opens doors to crime, despair, addiction, and injustice.

Can God call specific people to a season of simplicity for a higher purpose? Absolutely. Paul learned how to be content in much and in little, but contentment is not the same thing as celebrating poverty. Holiness comes by faith, not by lack. A holy people filled with the Spirit should be thriving in every area of life, including provision.

## Lie #17: Wanting increase is greedy.

Somehow we've been taught that even *wanting* more is sinful and that the moment you dream bigger, you're already in danger of idolatry. The Bible frames it differently. Jabez prayed, "Oh, that You would bless me indeed, and enlarge my territory" (1 Chron. 4:10), and God answered him. Jesus promised that those who give would receive blessings pressed down, shaken together, and running over. Solomon taught wisdom about multiplying resources and stewarding wealth.

Wanting increase isn't greedy when the increase serves the right purpose. You can't bless others if you have nothing to share or fund ministry if you can barely pay your own bills. Desire becomes greed only when it's self-serving, whereas desire for kingdom expansion remains sacred.

## Lie #18: Business was the devil's idea.

This one is laughable if you know history. Most people throughout biblical history were entrepreneurs: farmers, traders, and builders. The Proverbs 31 woman ran multiple streams of income including investments, manufacturing, real estate, and textiles. Jesus Himself likened His Father to a businessman who invests talents and expects a return.

Commerce isn't demonic; it's designed. Business, when built with

integrity and used for kingdom purposes, becomes one of the most powerful tools for discipling nations. It's time the church stopped viewing business as "secular" and started seeing it as sacred.

## Lie #19: Only rich people worship money.

This is another subtle deception. Some of the most money-obsessed
people I know are broke, living in constant anxiety about bills, missing
church because of work, and compromising their values chasing the next
paycheck. Worshipping money has nothing to do with how much you have
but everything to do with who you trust.

Jesus said no one can serve two masters: You cannot serve both God and
mammon. Some people bow to Pharaoh for a promotion while others bow
to Pharaoh just to survive, yet either way their allegiance is divided. The
goal isn't to have less money but to have more loyalty.

## Lie #20: You shouldn't give to get.

This one sounds spiritual and feels selfless, but it contradicts what
Jesus taught. Jesus said, "Give, and it will be given to you; good measure,
pressed down, shaken together, and running over will be put into your
bosom" (Luke 6:38). Paul said, "He who sows sparingly will also reap sparingly, and he who sows bountifully will also reap bountifully" (2 Cor. 9:6).
Malachi (3:10, NLT) says, "Test Me in this....See if I will not then open
the windows of heaven for you and pour out good things for you until
there is no more need." Proverbs (3:9–10, NIV) says, "Honor the LORD
with your wealth, with the firstfruits of all your crops; then your barns
will be filled to overflowing."

Giving doesn't make you greedy; it positions you for God's multiplication.

## Lie #21: You shouldn't make money serving God.

Some people act like making money while fulfilling your kingdom assignment is immoral, but should you make money serving the devil instead?
The Proverbs 31 woman prospered while honoring God, and David became
wealthy as he fought God's battles. Paul worked as a tentmaker for seasons,
yet even he said ministers are worthy of financial support and double honor.

Ministry isn't a vow of poverty; it's a call to stewardship. Psalm 1 says
if you meditate on the Word day and night, you will prosper. Joshua 1
says if you diligently obey, you will have good success. Ministry should be

a pathway to provision, not poverty. God doesn't bless ministers less; He expects His people to honor them more.

## Lie #22: There is such a thing as being "too rich."

People love to say things like, "Well, you can have just enough, but anything beyond that is dangerous." But where's the line? Is it a Honda Civic or a Corvette? A modest three-bedroom house or a five-bedroom one? The truth is, there's no biblical line that says, "This is the acceptable wealth level."

The Bible doesn't warn against having too much; it warns against trusting too much in what you have. Wealth is measured by stewardship, not morality. Solomon was unimaginably wealthy, and it pleased God to bless him. Abraham had enough livestock, silver, and gold to support hundreds of people. Job had double after his trial than he had before. God's issue is never how much you have but how much you trust. When wealth owns you, it's a curse; when you steward it faithfully, it becomes a blessing.

## Lie #23: God doesn't care about land or buildings.

Somehow we've convinced ourselves that God only cares about "spiritual things," as if property, real estate, and physical territory don't matter to Him. The God of the Bible shows otherwise. His covenants have always been connected to land. He promised Abraham territory for his descendants and led the Israelites into a Promised Land flowing with milk and honey. When Israel disobeyed, they lost land, not just spiritual blessings. When Jesus returns, He's not coming just for souls; He's coming to reign physically on a new earth.

Ownership matters in the kingdom. Spiritually speaking, demons occupy geographical territories, but when believers own the land, they can take authority over spiritual strongholds. That's why Nehemiah rebuilt the walls, Boaz owned the fields Ruth gleaned from, and the early church gathered in homes they owned. God cares about land and buildings because they are tools for establishing His kingdom on earth. They are not trophies for our glory but infrastructure for His.

# Conclusion

If you've believed any of these lies, you're not alone. So have I, and so has almost every believer at some point. The good news is that you don't have to stay bound by them. You can choose today to renew your mind, align your faith with the full counsel of Scripture, and reclaim the covenant promises Jesus paid for.

The world doesn't need another broke, bashful church. It needs a bold, resourced, Spirit-empowered church ready to fund the harvest, disciple nations, and flip the systems of the world upside down. This transformation starts with you, and it starts right now.

So ask yourself these questions: Which of these lies have you subconsciously agreed with in your thoughts, speech, or behaviors? How have those lies limited the way you earn, give, or expect God to provide? What truth from God's Word do you need to replace each lie with so you can live free and fruitful?

Pray this out loud:

> *Father, I thank You for exposing every lie that has kept me small, fearful, or ashamed of abundance. Today, I break agreement with every false belief that says poverty is holy, prosperity is evil, or increase is worldly. I reject every mindset that limits Your generosity in my life. You are my source, my provider, and my covenant-keeping God. I receive Your truth that You delight in the prosperity of Your servants and that You've given me power to create wealth in order to establish Your covenant on the earth. I renew my allegiance to You alone—not to mammon, not to fear, not to religion. From this day forward, my thoughts, words, and actions will align with heaven's economy. I will prosper Your way, for Your glory, and for the good of others. In Jesus' name, amen.*

To access additional resources, scan the QR code or visit thepowertoprosperbook.com/resources.

## CHAPTER 4

# THE SPIRIT OF MAMMON VERSUS THE SPIRIT OF GOD

A BATTLE IS HAPPENING over your finances, and it's not just about dollars and cents. It's about allegiance. Will you be directed by the spirit of mammon or by the Spirit of God?

I learned this the hard way. For years I had the cart before the horse while building a digital media agency and trying to sell my services to worldly clients. These weren't necessarily evil people, just partnerships God never told me to make. My dream was to focus on ministry full-time one day, going all in on creating content for the kingdom, but I believed the business needed to succeed first. I thought securing enough contracts and cash flow would finally justify doing what was really in my heart: launching a podcast.

God had other plans. He said to me, "Kap, your ministry doesn't need your business to be successful. Your business needs your ministry to be successful."

That revelation floored me. I realized I was treating ministry like a side project and business like the main thing, yet God wasn't going to bless it that way because He doesn't bless backward priorities.

Looking back, I can see how the spirit of mammon had subtly crept into my thinking. Mammon doesn't just manifest in greed or obvious idolatry. Sometimes it disguises itself as "wisdom" or "responsibility." It whispers, "Just get the bag first, secure the deal first, then you'll have the freedom to do what God's put in your heart." This sounds logical, but it's rebellion dressed up in respectability.

Here's the real nature of mammon: It isn't money but a lying spirit, the false god that tempts you to trust in wealth instead of the voice of God. Jesus said you can't serve both God and mammon (Matt. 6:24). He didn't even say you can't serve both God and Satan but mammon, because mammon is one of Satan's most seductive tools. Mammon promises security without surrender, provision without relationship, tricking you into thinking your ability to survive depends on your own hustle instead of heaven's help.

The trap works like this: Mammon wants you to believe you can figure it out without God's daily voice, that you can fund your assignment in your own strength and build your future without fresh obedience. You can't. Mammon wants you to live by formulas while God wants you to live by faith.

When I finally went all in on ministry and stopped using business as a safety net by simply doing what God told me to do, everything changed. 2023 became the most prosperous year of my life not because I chased money harder but because I prioritized the mission. I created content God told me to create, focusing on cultural commentary and reaction videos not because they were my personal preference but because God said, "This is the field where I want you." When I obeyed, He breathed on it, taking my YouTube channel from a thousand to over a million subscribers in a year. He blessed my business without me chasing it because I wasn't chasing provision but obedience.

Obedience is not a onetime decision but a daily dependence. Somewhere along the way, after success came, I got comfortable and started trusting the method instead of the Master. I knew the formula worked and what kind of content the algorithm liked. "Why change what's working?" I thought. Even when my heart wasn't fully in it anymore, I kept running the play. That's when I missed it.

The spirit of mammon isn't just about chasing money. It's about staying stuck in what *used* to work because you're too afraid to trust God for what's next, clinging to an old blessing after God's hand has moved on. This is how mammon enslaves believers who once started in faith.

At the end of 2024, God used a series of disruptions to get my attention. My whole family got violently sick, I slipped a disc in my back and couldn't walk, and every plan I had collapsed. I realized I was no longer sensitive to the voice that brought me here. I was coasting, surviving on yesterday's word. In that place of pain and repentance, God reminded me: Dependence is daily, sensitivity to the Spirit is not optional, and provision isn't found in repeating old formulas but in following fresh instructions.

God led me to Isaiah 54:2–3:

Enlarge the place of your tent, and let them stretch out the curtains of your dwellings; do not spare; lengthen your cords, and strengthen your stakes. For you shall expand to the right and to the left.

God wasn't calling me to protect the blessing I already had. He was calling me to build an addition and to spare no expense. He was preparing me for new growth, new harvest, new influence, yet He couldn't fill what I hadn't built. I had to move first, to stretch in faith.

God told me to launch a new YouTube channel. Even though I had just reached a million subscribers on the first one, He said, "Build another net. Create another boat. Prepare for the overflow." It didn't make sense in the natural, costing money and time, but I obeyed. Within months, that second channel began growing faster than my first one ever had.

This is what it means to serve the Spirit of God over the spirit of mammon. Mammon says, "Protect what you have," while God says, "Prepare for what's coming." Mammon says, "Play it safe," while God says, "Stretch wider." Mammon says, "Repeat the formula," while God says, "Follow the cloud."

Following the Spirit of God doesn't mean you abandon stewardship or throw strategy out the window. It means putting kingdom metrics first. Your ultimate KPI (key performance indicator) is no longer clicks, cash, or clout but souls, obedience, and prayer. Ironically, when you prioritize God's priorities, He trusts you with more.

Let me share a story that illustrates why this matters so much. I saw a Christian content creator who built his whole platform on mocking other believers, especially those who taught about prosperity. He made jokes about pastors who preached about blessing, called out Christians who talked about wealth, and rooted his entire brand in criticizing what he didn't understand. A few months later, he posted on Instagram asking for financial help, literally dropping his digital payment link saying he needed support.

I was about to send him something out of genuine compassion when I felt a check in my spirit. The Holy Spirit seemed to say, "Don't sow into that. He's not struggling just because of circumstance but because he's dishonored what I wanted to bless." It hit me: When you despise prosperity in your heart, you disqualify yourself from receiving it. You can't mock harvest and expect to reap it, bash blessed believers and then wonder why you're stuck. You have to honor the principles of God if you want to walk in the provision of God.

## False Humility Is Still Loyalty to Mammon

One of the most dangerous ways the spirit of mammon works in the church is by disguising itself as false humility. It doesn't just whisper to rich people, "Trust your wealth." It whispers to believers stuck in lack, "Stay small. Play it safe. Don't ask for too much. Don't dream too big." This sounds spiritual and feels like piety, but it's really fear in disguise. At the root it's still about self-preservation and keeping yourself in control.

Real humility doesn't resist blessing. Real humility says, "God, whatever You want to pour out, I'll receive it, and I'll steward it for Your glory." If the enemy can't get you to bow to greed, he'll get you to bow to limitation. Either way, you stay ineffective.

## Judging Prosperity Blocks Your Own Blessing

Another trap the spirit of mammon sets is getting you to judge people who walk in the blessing you secretly desire. You see someone prospering righteously, building businesses, discipling leaders, funding ministries, and instead of celebrating, you start critiquing. You assume they must be greedy, compromised, or manipulating people, thus sabotaging your own harvest.

Jesus said plainly: With the measure you use, it will be measured back to you. If you honor prosperity done God's way, you position yourself to receive it, but if you resent it, you repel it. If you constantly accuse every blessed believer of corruption, don't be surprised when you stay stuck in cycles of lack. Honor what you want to attract, celebrate what you want God to multiply in your life, and stop judging what you don't understand. You can't inherit what you secretly despise.

## Broke but Busy: Mammon's Favorite Deception

Most Christians think mammon only grips rich people, but the truth is mammon loves using broke people too. Mammon doesn't care how much you have; it cares about who you trust. For many believers, the spirit of mammon has kept them broke but busy. They've been hustling, grinding, worrying, and working two or three jobs just to make ends meet. Yet they still live in fear, constantly anxious about money, stressed about provision, and always thinking about the next check, bill, or crisis.

This isn't freedom. It's slavery, and just as much bondage as greed. Mammon will keep you exhausted in survival mode so you never step into abundance, making you think you're "humble" because you don't have much. In reality, you're still trusting in your own strength to provide instead of the God who said He would teach you to profit. You can be broke and still bowing to mammon because freedom isn't about having less or more but about allegiance.

I've seen this principle work not just in my own life but in the lives of others who are choosing the Spirit of God over the spirit of mammon. My friends Kevin and Bree watched their ministry explode when they stopped measuring success by financial metrics and started measuring it by hours spent in prayer. My friend Andy, one of the most successful sales trainers in the world, shifted his entire company culture to focus not just on crushing revenue goals but on winning souls and discipling people through business. The blessing hasn't stopped; it's multiplied.

That's how the kingdom works.

Jesus said, "Make friends for yourselves by means of unrighteous wealth" (Luke 16:9, ESV). In other words, money isn't the goal but the tool, and when you use it for kingdom purposes, you turn temporary wealth into eternal reward.

Paul reinforced the same truth in 1 Timothy 6:17–19:

> Command those who are rich in this present age not to be haughty, nor to trust in uncertain riches but in the living God, who gives us richly all things to enjoy. Let them do good, that they be rich in good works, ready to give, willing to share, storing up for themselves a good foundation for the time to come.

God doesn't mind you enjoying wealth. He minds you trusting in it.

If you've been stuck financially, frustrated spiritually, or exhausted emotionally, this is your wake-up call. Break agreement with the spirit of mammon. Break agreement with scarcity. Break agreement with the lie that provision depends on you. Choose today to walk in the Spirit of God, the One who teaches you to profit, leads you in the way you should go, and delights in prospering His children when they prioritize His purposes.

Consecrate your business, dreams, finances back to Him. Bring every spreadsheet, product, paycheck, and plan, and lay it at His feet. Let Him be the director again. Let Him lead you again—and watch what happens when heaven backs your obedience.

You weren't made to strive for scraps. You were made to steward kingdom wealth, to collaborate with your Father. You were made for more.

Let's move forward in freedom.

To access additional resources, scan the QR code or visit thepowertoprosperbook. com/resources.

# PART II
# THE PROMISE OF PROSPERITY

## CHAPTER 5

# THE PATTERN OF PROSPERITY

PROSPERITY DIDN'T BEGIN with Abraham or start in Deuteronomy. It wasn't first introduced in Proverbs or promised through Paul. *It began in Eden.* From the very beginning, prosperity was built into the DNA of creation. God didn't create Adam and Eve in a place of lack or put them in a desert saying, "Try to survive." Instead, He placed them in a garden filled with abundance: trees of every kind, rivers flowing with gold and precious stones, and provision built into the landscape. Fruitfulness was never a reward we earned through obedience but a natural result of relationship with God.

Genesis 2 describes the Garden of Eden not just as a paradise but as a place of overflowing resources where humanity could walk with God, steward creation, cultivate beauty, and live in unbroken peace. This wasn't scarcity but surplus, and none of it was accidental. The original atmosphere of humanity was prosperity, telling us something important: Lack was never God's plan.

Lack came with the fall, poverty with sin, scarcity as a result of the curse, but not Eden. In Eden there was no toil, no anxiety about bills, no scraping to get ahead, and no fear of not having enough. Adam didn't work to survive; he worked from abundance. His assignment was to tend and keep what was already overflowing. His job wasn't to hustle for provision but to steward what God had already generously provided.

This matters because too many Christians believe prosperity is a modern invention or, even worse, a worldly perversion, simply because they've forgotten Eden. Before disobedience, before sin, before even a need for redemption, there was prosperity. That was the starting point, the original ecosystem of man and God. If you don't start there, you'll misinterpret the entire storyline of blessing, treating overflow as if it's optional and abundance like it's suspicious. When you remember Eden, you remember that prosperity was God's idea first.

That's why the pattern of prosperity runs so deeply through Scripture, because God has always been trying to restore what was lost in Eden. Not just spiritually but practically, tangibly, and economically.

When you study Scripture carefully, a pattern emerges that's neither random nor accidental. A pattern that reveals the heart of God over and over again: God delights in prospering His people.

I want Christians everywhere to see this is not some American invention, not a capitalist invention, and not a modern marketing ploy from preachers in Houston or Dallas. You would have to read your Bible with your eyes closed to ignore the pattern. Prosperity starts in Eden, saturates the life of God's covenant people, and shows up in the kingdom of heaven even now. It climaxes with the new heaven and new earth where there is no lack, no death, no sorrow—only abundance forever. If you think prosperity is a modern idea, you're missing the original design of the garden and the eternal destiny of the redeemed.

From Genesis to Revelation, the evidence is overwhelming. God doesn't just want His people spiritually strong; He wants them resourced, empowered, and established to fulfill their assignments. Financial prosperity was never meant to be a side issue but was woven into the covenant from the beginning.

You can trace it all the way back to Abraham, called by God to leave his homeland and follow Him into an unknown future. What did God promise him? Not just descendants or a legacy but blessing. Tangible blessing. In Genesis 13:2, it says, "Abram was very rich in livestock, in silver, and in gold." God didn't apologize for it. He initiated it. Prosperity was part of Abraham's covenant relationship with God.

The pattern continued with Isaac. When famine struck the land, Isaac chose to sow seed anyway. While the world around him was collapsing economically, Isaac increased—the man began to prosper, continued prospering, and became very prosperous. That wasn't coincidence but covenant.

Jacob followed the same trajectory. God blessed the work of his hands so powerfully that even when his employer, Laban, tried to cheat him out of his wages, Jacob still multiplied. He left Laban's household not empty-handed but with abundant flocks, herds, and wealth.

Joseph's story is another undeniable testimony. Betrayed by his brothers, sold into slavery, and thrown into prison, yet because God's favor was on him, Joseph rose to become second-in-command over all Egypt. Pharaoh entrusted Joseph with the nation's entire economic system because the prosperity of the covenant rested on him, even in a foreign land.

The pattern isn't just about individuals. Deuteronomy 28:2 lays it out explicitly for the entire nation of Israel: "And all these blessings shall come upon you and overtake you, because you obey the voice of the LORD your God." It lists blessing after blessing: prosperity in your fields, livestock, children, and storehouses. God makes it plain. Obedience positions you for overflow.

After Moses's death, God commissioned Joshua to lead Israel into the Promised Land, telling him:

> This Book of the Law shall not depart from your mouth, but you shall meditate in it day and night...for then you will make your way prosperous, and then you will have good success.
>
> —JOSHUA 1:8

Prosperity was directly tied to covenant obedience.

Job's story is often misunderstood because of his season of suffering, but most people forget how the story ends: "Now the LORD blessed the latter days of Job more than his beginning" (Job 42:12). God restored Job's fortunes and gave him double. Prosperity wasn't canceled; it was magnified.

Consider the widows ministered to by Elijah and Elisha. Both women were on the brink of financial and literal death, but when they obeyed the prophetic instruction to sow what little they had into the kingdom, supernatural provision flooded their homes. The oil multiplied, the flour didn't run out, their debts were paid, their lives were saved. God didn't scold them for needing financial miracles; He performed them.

King David, a man after God's own heart, wasn't just a worshipper and a warrior; he was wildly blessed. He stockpiled immense wealth to fund the building of the temple, even though he knew he wouldn't live to see it completed. David understood that prosperity wasn't about personal luxury but about generational legacy.

Solomon, David's son, asked God for wisdom, and God responded by giving him not only wisdom but wealth beyond anything the world had ever seen: "King Solomon surpassed all the kings of the earth in riches and wisdom" (1 Kings 10:23). Wisdom brought wealth, not as a curse but as a crowning.

Even obscure characters like Obed-Edom testify to the pattern of prosperity. When the ark of the covenant (the very presence of God) rested in his house, Obed-Edom's household exploded with blessing (2 Sam. 6:11). God's presence attracts provision.

The wisdom literature reinforces this pattern again and again. Proverbs 3:9–10 says,

> Honor the LORD with your possessions, and with the firstfruits of all your increase; so your barns will be filled with plenty, and your vats will overflow with new wine.

That's not a vague hope but a guaranteed outcome for those who put God first.

Malachi 3:10 delivers a similar promise. God challenges His people to bring the full tithe into the storehouse and says,

> Try Me now in this…if I will not open for you the windows of heaven and pour out for you such blessing that there will not be room enough to receive it.

God's blessing isn't about scraping by. It's about surplus.

Even the minor prophet Haggai calls the people out for neglecting God's house while building their own luxury homes, linking their financial struggle directly to misplaced priorities: "You earn wages, only to put them in a purse with holes in it" (Hag. 1:6, NIV). The solution wasn't to demonize prosperity but to align with God's purposes again.

In the New Testament the pattern continues through the life and ministry of Jesus. When Peter obeyed Jesus and cast his nets one more time, his fishing business experienced an overflow so massive that both boats began to sink. Jesus wasn't punishing Peter for working; He was blessing Peter for obeying. Jesus also demonstrated supernatural provision when He multiplied five loaves and two fish to feed thousands, with baskets of leftovers. Not just barely enough but more than enough.

Jesus didn't just model prosperity; He taught it. Again, He said,

> Give, and it will be given to you: good measure, pressed down, shaken together, and running over will be put into your bosom.
>
> —LUKE 6:38

He taught that the same measure you use in generosity is the measure that will come back to you, that if you seek first the kingdom of God and

His righteousness, "all these things" (food, clothing, provision) will "be added unto you" (Matt. 6:33, KJV). He promised that those who sacrificed for the gospel would receive "a hundredfold now in this time…and in the age to come, eternal life" (Mark 10:29–30). Jesus didn't say "maybe." He didn't say "only in heaven." He said, "*in this time*…with persecutions" (v. 30, emphasis added). Prosperity and persecution often walk together.

Jesus also affirmed that those who labor in the work of the kingdom are worthy of their wages (Luke 10:7). Ministry wasn't meant to be a path to poverty but was designed to be sustained by the very provision God promises.

Paul picked up the same thread. In 2 Corinthians 9 he wrote, "He who sows sparingly will also reap sparingly, and he who sows bountifully will also reap bountifully" (v. 6). God isn't stingy; His grace abounds toward the generous. Paul also instructed Timothy that "the elders who rule well [should] be counted worthy of double honor, especially those who labor in the word and doctrine" (1 Tim. 5:17). In other words, kingdom workers weren't supposed to scrape by but to be honored doubly.

John the apostle, late in his life, echoed the same heart when he wrote to the beloved Gaius: "Beloved, I pray that you may prosper in all things and be in health, just as your soul prospers" (3 John 2). Prosperity wasn't limited to the spiritual realm but meant to touch every part of life.

The pattern is clear, consistent, and covenantal. God delights in the prosperity of His people, not so they can hoard wealth but so they can fulfill their purposes. He blesses them not to build monuments to themselves or chase after stuff but to fund movements for His glory and pursue souls with every resource they've been entrusted with. Prosperity isn't a side issue. It's a covenant confirmation.

It's time for the church to stop being embarrassed about it and start walking in it because the pattern of prosperity isn't man-made but God-ordained, waiting for those who will believe Him enough to receive it.

To access additional resources, scan the QR code or visit thepowertoprosperbook.com/resources.

CHAPTER 6

# GOD'S COVENANT INCLUDES WEALTH

MOST CHRISTIANS BELIEVE God wants to save their souls. Some believe He wants to heal their bodies. But few believe deep down that God actually wants to prosper them.

Let's go straight to the foundation in Deuteronomy 8:18: "You shall remember the LORD your God, for it is He who gives you power to get wealth, that He may establish His covenant." Notice this scripture doesn't say God gives you wealth to test your character, tempt your pride, or even see how much you can give away. It says plainly He does this so that He might establish His covenant.

Let that sink in. Wealth is not just a blessing but a covenantal assignment.

God's covenant with Abraham included land, descendants, and generational wealth. Galatians 3 makes it clear: "If you are Christ's, then you are Abraham's seed, and heirs according to the promise" (v. 29). This means the covenant God made with Abraham is your inheritance spiritually, metaphorically, and materially.

The same God who brought Abraham out of Ur with a promise is bringing you out of debt, fear, and survival mode into fruitfulness and financial authority. His covenant promises are explicit: "You shall lend... but you shall not borrow" (Deut. 28:12). "Your barns will be filled with plenty" (Prov. 3:10). "Wealth and riches will be in [your] house" (Ps. 112:3). "You will eat the fruit of your labor; blessings and prosperity will be yours" (Ps. 128:2, NIV). "He became poor, that you through His poverty might become rich" (2 Cor. 8:9).

This isn't prosperity theory but prosperity covenant, and like any covenant, it comes with conditions.

# We've Forgotten the Power of Covenant

Many believers struggle with Deuteronomy 8:18 because we no longer understand covenant power. Covenant isn't just a "nice idea" in the kingdom but the highest form of commitment, an unbreakable bond. Today, most people treat covenant like it's optional, like a mere suggestion, approaching it like modern marriage vows based on feelings rather than faithfulness. When challenges arise, we walk away, bail when uncomfortable, and treat promises as disposable. Our casual approach to our own word will project that same attitude onto God.

God operates differently. He never breaks His promises or renegotiates His Word because culture changed or circumstances hardened. When God makes a covenant, He doesn't flinch, fold, or blink. He binds Himself to His Word and honors it completely.

Psalm 138:2 declares, "You have magnified Your word above all Your name." Think about that. God's own name, His reputation and glory, stands second to His Word's authority. This demonstrates how seriously He takes His promises. God holds His Word above His reputation because His Word is His reputation.

Isaiah 55:11 affirms,

> So shall My word be that goes forth from My mouth; it shall not return to Me void, but it shall accomplish what I please, and it shall prosper in the thing for which I sent it.

When God speaks, the matter is finished. Scripture presents this not as a wish or pleasant thought but as an accomplishment that prospers in its purpose, never fizzling halfway or returning empty. It hits the target every time.

Jeremiah 1:12 states, "I am watching over My word to perform it." God remains fully engaged with His promises. He is not distant or uncertain about their fulfillment. Instead, He actively oversees His Word—guarding it, protecting it, and bringing it to pass, as the covenant-keeping God He is.

Proverbs 30:5–6 teaches,

> Every word of God is pure; He is a shield to those who put their trust in Him. Do not add to His words, lest He rebuke you, and you be found a liar.

Every divine word remains flawless. It's never impure, exaggerated, or uncertain. God views the twisting of, minimizing of, and addition to His Word with serious displeasure because His Word needs no editing. It simply needs believing.

Deuteronomy 8:18 ties directly to this truth: God's covenant to prosper His people reveals His integrity rather than indulgence, proving to the world that He keeps His promises. "You shall remember the LORD your God, for it is He who gives you power to get wealth, that He may establish His covenant."

God doesn't bless you just so you can be comfortable. He blesses you to reveal His faithfulness and to put His covenant on display. When people see your life, they witness a living testimony of His goodness and know He's a God who keeps His word.

Understanding this truth changes everything. We would stop treating prosperity like a maybe. We would stop apologizing for wanting to increase and stop acting like believing God for financial blessing is greedy or worldly. It's not. It's biblical. It's covenantal. It's part of the deal.

God is asking you not to chase after money but to trust Him enough to steward it. He's asking you to believe that when He said He would bless the work of your hands, He meant it. The prosperity He promised isn't a side benefit but a covenant confirmation. When you understand the weight God puts on His Word, you won't wonder whether His promises apply to you. You'll realize they're waiting for you.

## Covenant over Luck

Many Christians are still waiting for a breakthrough for which God has already provided the blueprint. They're hoping for a random check in the mail, a stranger to cover their rent, or a miracle they can post about. Covenant doesn't work like that.

Covenant is not luck. It's law. It's a spiritual contract that activates God's power when you align with His terms. If you're struggling to believe this, consider these questions: Why would God command tithing if He didn't intend to bless those who tithe (Mal. 3:10–11)? Why would Jesus say, "Give, and it will be given to you" if He didn't mean it (Luke 6:38)? Why would Proverbs say, "Honor the LORD with your wealth...then your barns will be filled" if it were untrue (3:9–10, NIV)?

God's financial system runs on governing principles rather than guess-work. If you sow, you reap. If you steward, you're trusted. If you tithe, you're covered. If you give, you're blessed. This represents partnership rather than performance. You're moving in sync with God rather than manipulating Him.

## My Turning Point

I remember the season when I was asking God to bless my business but nothing was working. I was trying everything in the natural: networking, building funnels, studying strategy. I had the skill set, but the break-through wouldn't come.

One day in frustration I cried out, "God, what gives? I'm trying to do this for You!"

His response was clear: "Kap, I'm not obligated to bless your version of My vision for your business."

That moment changed everything. I had the covenant in theory but not in practice. I wasn't truly remembering the Lord my God. Instead, I was leaning on my own understanding, building my business with Christian language but carnal strategy. Even though I was doing good things, I wasn't aligned with His instructions.

My shift came when I prioritized Him in my time, attention, and finances. Everything started changing—not instantly or effortlessly but producing consistent and sustainable fruit.

## The Prosperity Resistance

This explains why there's so much warfare around the topic of prosperity. It's not just a theological debate but a spiritual battle. Satan knows that if you embrace the covenant, you'll become dangerous. Money in the hands of a righteous person becomes a weapon against hell, and a funded believer can create media, rescue kids, plant churches, and disciple nations.

Satan has worked overtime to corrupt the message and confuse the church, making us think it's holier to be broke. He's made us afraid of wealth because of what it might "do to us," and he's convinced us that ambition equals idolatry. Scripture counters this deception: "Let the

Lord be magnified, Who takes pleasure in the prosperity of His servant" (Ps. 35:27, AMPC).

You never have to apologize for wanting to increase or have to shrink back because others think it's "too much." When you understand this is covenant and not personal indulgence, you stop making excuses and start making an impact.

God desires not only to bless you but to trust you, and when He trusts you, He funds you.

To access additional resources, scan the QR code or visit thepowertoprosperbook. com/resources.

## CHAPTER 7

# DON'T GO BACK TO EGYPT

WHEN GOD DELIVERED Israel out of Egypt, He didn't just rescue them from slavery. He invited them into covenant prosperity. Yet as soon as things got tough in the wilderness, what did they do? They begged to go back to Pharaoh, back to slavery, back to the very place they had cried to be delivered from.

Why would they choose this? Because *Pharaoh was predictable.* Sure, he abused them, but at least they knew what to expect. Yeah, he kept them poor, but they got fed. Even though they were oppressed, at least they didn't have to walk by faith.

It's easy to criticize the Israelites for their unbelief, but most believers today still operate with a Pharaoh mindset. They'd rather have a guaranteed paycheck than build something from scratch, be told what to do rather than take initiative, and depend on broken systems rather than live by kingdom principles.

They might have been saved out of Egypt, but Egypt still lives within them, and Pharaoh loves it that way. He delights when believers settle for just enough and when Christians feel spiritual about playing it small while the church stays dependent on Egypt's economy, too scared to step into God's.

God didn't just bring you out of bondage. He's leading you into the promised land. Deuteronomy 6:10–12 (NIV) declares,

> When the LORD your God brings you into the land he swore to your fathers...with large, flourishing cities you did not build, houses filled with all kinds of good things...wells you did not dig, and vineyards and olive groves you did not plant—then when you eat and are satisfied, be careful that you do not forget the LORD, who brought you out of Egypt, out of the land of slavery.

Prosperity is harder to manage than bondage. Bondage tells you what to do, whereas prosperity gives you options. With options comes responsibility.

Many Christians shrink back, not because they don't love God but because they're terrified of managing the freedom He's offering.

I experienced this struggle personally. When God called me to surrender my agency and fully commit to kingdom content, it made no financial sense. I knew how to hustle but had no clue how to trust. That season exposed my Pharaoh mindset as I looked to my own systems instead of His covenant for security.

When financial pressure hits, do you look to God or back to Pharaoh? Modern-day Pharaohs appear in many forms:

+ the job you refuse to leave despite God's direction to start something new

+ the system you rely on instead of developing your God-given gifts

+ the employer you trust more than Jehovah Jireh

+ the credit card you reach for before praying

+ the safe career path you accept although God gave you a blueprint for impact

+ the business idea you shelve because the market looks too competitive

+ the relationships you maintain out of fear rather than faith

Today's Pharaoh is anything that offers false safety while keeping you stuck. A Pharaoh is any system that gives you just enough to survive while stealing your capacity to thrive.

## The Mark of the Beast Versus the Mark of Covenant

This is where this topic takes a dark turn.

Many Christians today would rather take the mark of the beast than learn to walk in covenant provision. Sound dramatic? Consider this: In Deuteronomy 6 we see God tell His people to bind His Word on their *foreheads and hands*. In Revelation 13 the Antichrist forces people to take a mark on their *foreheads and hands*. Both marks represent *covenant allegiance*.

The mark of the beast isn't just some microchip or barcode; it's a decision to trust a false system to survive. It represents economic allegiance. The only people who will resist that mark in the future are those who already know how to live by God's economy now. Without learning to live by covenant principles today, you become vulnerable when pressure increases.

God's warning to Israel makes perfect sense: "Remember the LORD your God, for it is He who gives you power to get wealth" (Deut. 8:18). This instruction isn't just so you can prosper but so you don't get enslaved again. Prosperity creates freedom, yet freedom demands faith.

God didn't call you out of Egypt just to wander in the wilderness. He called you to occupy the land, own property, influence cities, feed nations, and break generational bondage.

What does refusing to return to Pharaoh actually look like? It means

+ building what God directed you to build even when it seems illogical,

+ saying no to quick money when God instructs you to wait for clean money,

+ launching the business God revealed during prayer despite others mocking you,

+ refusing to manipulate or compromise to get ahead,

+ tithing and giving even when it feels tight,

+ turning down a higher-paying position that distracts from your assignment,

+ and declaring God's Word over your finances when fear tries to grip you.

Let God expose every place in your heart that still prefers Pharaoh. Then let Him break that Pharaoh because there's *no going back*—only forward. The promised land is waiting.

## Genesis 26: Don't Run to Egypt When Things Get Hard

To understand what it truly means to resist returning to Egypt's systems, we need to examine Isaac's story in Genesis 26 carefully. This passage illustrates the choice between worldly wisdom and kingdom faith during times of crisis.

During a severe famine, Isaac's first instinct was to go to Abimelech, king of the Philistines, in Gerar. Sound familiar? Like many Christians today, his impulse during crisis was to seek help from worldly leadership. When financial difficulties arise, our first impulse often drives us toward banks for loans, wealthy family members, or government assistance—to anywhere but God first.

God stepped in with clear instructions:

> Do not go down to Egypt; live in the land of *which I shall tell you.* Dwell in this land, and I will be with you and bless you; for to you and your descendants I give all these lands, and I will perform the oath which I swore to Abraham your father.
> —GENESIS 26:2–3, EMPHASIS ADDED

Don't buy the lie that you need to chase opportunity in places that look more prosperous. That's the same worldly thinking that destroyed Lot's family. He walked by *sight* instead of *faith*. True faith means living according to God's Word. Moving somewhere because you think it's logically better is living in "a way that seems right to a man, but its end is the way of death" (Prov. 14:12).

Go where God is calling you to go. He is not obligated to bless you in a place He never assigned to you. God promised Isaac, "I will be with you" (Gen. 26:3). God's presence generates power for prosperity. It's not just your gifting, wisdom, or connections; it's God's very presence in your life that *creates* the blessing.

Look at what happened when the ark of the covenant was in Obed-Edom's house: Everything prospered just because God's presence was there. The divine presence itself produced blessing. Same with Joseph. God was with him, and everything he touched prospered, even in prison and slavery. When God is with you, you become like a tree planted by the riverside, bearing fruit in *every season* regardless of your circumstances.

God promised Isaac *lands* because land ownership appears throughout Scripture; it matters to God. If it didn't, He wouldn't have included it in so many covenants with His people. "I will perform the oath..." (Gen. 26:3) demonstrates God's relentless commitment to His own integrity. Again, Psalm 138:2 says God exalts His Word above His own name. If His Word means nothing, His name means nothing.

## Prosperity Despite Famine

Then Isaac obeyed. Here's what happened:

> Then Isaac sowed in that land, and reaped in the same year a hundredfold; and the LORD blessed him. The man began to prosper, and continued prospering until he became very prosperous; for he had possessions of flocks and possessions of herds and a great number of servants. So the Philistines envied him.
>
> —GENESIS 26:12–14

Isaac sowed seed in the middle of famine. The famine was irrelevant because Isaac occupied the land God called him to. He obeyed God's voice instead of looking for handouts from King Abimelech. Rather than following worldly wisdom to relocate somewhere that looked more promising, he planted where God planted him, and God rewarded him a hundredfold.

The progression is beautiful: He "began to prosper, and continued prospering until he became very prosperous" (v. 13). Some people argue, "Isaac's prosperity wasn't material. God promises only spiritual prosperity." What about the very next words? Scripture says God prospered him, "*for he had possessions*" (v. 14, emphasis added). This proves God's blessing in Isaac's life was both spiritual and material!

After Isaac prospered, the Philistines envied him. This pattern repeats consistently. Lawsuits don't target struggling mom-and-pop shops; they go after thriving businesses because there's better financial reward. Proverbs teaches this: "The ransom of a man's life is his riches, but the poor does not hear rebuke" (13:8).

Jesus confirmed this truth:

> Assuredly, I say to you, there is no one who has left house or brothers or sisters or father or mother or wife or children or lands, for My sake and the gospel's, who shall not receive a *hundredfold now in this time*—houses and brothers and sisters and mothers and children and lands, *with persecutions*—and in the age to come, eternal life.
> —MARK 10:29–30, EMPHASIS ADDED

Does every Jesus follower get their name on a hundred house deeds? Probably not, and honestly, that wouldn't be a blessing for most people. Can you imagine a hundred property tax bills, utility payments, and lawns to mow? You can't even live in them all at once.

When you operate by kingdom principles, God ensures your needs are met while granting unmerited favor you couldn't fight for yourself. Think about Acts 2, when the disciples sold everything and shared with one another. Through everyone's generosity nobody had just one or two properties—everyone had access to dozens, maybe hundreds. God's presence created favor that gave them access to resources they didn't personally own.

When Jesus told His disciples not to pack supplies for ministry trips, He was demonstrating kingdom reality: When you commit to God's work, His favor provides in ways you can't manufacture yourself. They gained access to homes and properties not through manipulation or begging but because God's presence opened doors.

Consider when God promised the Israelites they would occupy homes they didn't build—a divine transfer of resources. Sometimes stewardship beats ownership. Owners deal with problems stewards don't face. There are things God wants to bless you with that are actually more enjoyable when they flow through your hands than when you clutch them tightly.

Besides, you can't take any of it with you when you die. God owns "the cattle on a thousand hills" (Ps. 50:10). Earth is His footstool. Everything belongs to Him anyway. What you "own" is ultimately God's, entrusted to you momentarily for His purposes—just like the man with the brand-new colt who immediately released it when Jesus said, "The Lord needs it"

(Luke 19:34, NIV; see also vv. 30–33, 35). That man understood the colt wasn't even his to begin with.

This reminds me of when I was in the middle of the building season of my brand. Before we had a breakthrough financially, we had a breakthrough of favor. We have some friends who have been blessed with an extremely successful business selling orthopedics, and one day, they invited my wife and me on a fully paid vacation to Cabo, Mexico, in one the most luxurious resorts we've ever stayed in. This is just one of many stories where God's principles of prosperity followed us simply because we sought first the kingdom of God.

So it amazes me when people argue, "Jesus never promised prosperity. He promised suffering and persecution!" Actually, He promised both prosperity and persecution, and in the same verse! The prospering favor of God over a believer's life will produce persecution. Guaranteed.

Look at Jesus as the prime example. His life perfectly radiated God's favor everywhere He went. How did religious leaders without that same blessing respond? With pure envy. They hated that this man moved with grace, ease, and power they couldn't study their way into. They resented that people preferred His company over theirs and despised how everywhere He went, He was welcomed and served. They couldn't stand how people humbled themselves before His teaching and how followers literally poured out resources and life savings to support His ministry and honor Him personally.

Their jealousy led to the most remarkable persecution imaginable: the crucifixion of the Son of God.

Consider Judas, treasurer of Jesus' ministry. When Mary poured expensive perfume at Jesus' feet in worship, Judas immediately complained, "She could've sold that and given the money to the poor" (John 12:4–5, paraphrased). How righteous of you, Judas—the same man who would sell his own Savior to murderers for thirty pieces of silver. The spirit of mammon works particularly in partnership with the spirit of religion, demanding financial standards from others while exempting itself.

If Judas had been truly free from the spirit of mammon, he would've celebrated Mary's worship and remembered that money comes and goes (Prov. 27:24). Instead, treasure consumed way too much space in his heart.

His subjective judgment about proper use of resources erupted in anger and self-righteousness, leading to the most horrific downfall imaginable: trading God for a quick buck.

Now let's take a look at how this plays out in our modern context. As I've mentioned, when you're just running a mom-and-pop shop, the likelihood of you facing a lawsuit is very low. But when your company is making a ton of money and your enemies want a piece of the harvest you worked hard for, you're going to need to start budgeting for legal counsel and even legal insurance. It's just like the Proverb that says, "The ransom of a man's life is his riches, but the poor does not hear rebuke" (13:8, MEV).

To access additional resources, scan the QR code or visit thepowertoprosperbook.com/resources.

# PART III

# THE POWER FOR PROSPERITY

## CHAPTER 8

# THE LAW OF THE WORD

PROSPERITY STARTS WORKING the moment the truth replaces the lie. The first two sections of this book served that purpose. We confronted the bad theology that kept God's people small, hesitant, and ashamed of increase. Now it's time to rebuild. This section is about reprogramming your mind with the laws that actually govern the anointing for prosperity.

These laws are real. They operate with or without your permission. They are as predictable as gravity. You don't have to agree with gravity for it to pull you to the ground. In the same way, the laws that govern kingdom wealth don't bend to emotions, opinions, or tradition. They simply work for those who work them.

These laws are not the full list. Scripture is filled with layered patterns, principles, and precepts. But the laws you are about to study carry enough force to create undeniable momentum in your financial life. Apply them consistently and you will not stay where you are.

Think of these laws like the mechanical system of a car. Some people tithe and still wonder why they're stuck. That's like filling the gas tank and then getting confused when the car won't start because the battery is dead or a spark plug is shot. One working component cannot override the ones that are out of order. But when everything is aligned, that vehicle moves with power.

As you work through these chapters, slow down. Let the truth settle. Fill out every reflection question. Don't skip the prayer at the end. Speak it out loud. Engage your faith. Activate your expectation. The goal isn't information. The goal is transformation that shows up in your life.

Ready? Let's begin.

~~~~~

There's a reason Satan's first attack on humanity began with one question: "Did God really say...?" (Gen. 3:1, NIV). It wasn't just a challenge to God's authority; it was an attack on His Word. The enemy knows that if you don't know what's written, you'll settle for whatever someone else says.

I learned this lesson the hard—and funny—way on a trip to Nashville.

My video guy and I were flying back after producing a podcast shoot, and we had what felt like a hundred pounds of camera gear between us. Our bags were loaded down: tripods, lights, lenses, you name it. But thankfully, we had media passes, which meant we were supposed to be exempt from overweight baggage fees.

We rolled up to the airline counter, showed them our credentials, and said, "Hey, we're checking media equipment—these should be covered."

The attendant looked at our passes and said, "Oh, that only works for NBC, CNN, or other large broadcast networks."

We kind of laughed. "No," I said, "that's not what your policy says."

She doubled down. "Sorry, sir, that's the rule."

So I pulled up the airline's website right there on my phone, scrolled to the section labeled Media Baggage Policy, and showed her—word for word—that it applied to any commercial media production company, not just major networks.

She blinked, excused herself, and went to talk to her manager. A few minutes later, she came back and said, "OK...this time, we'll let it slide."

We smiled and said, "Sure. This time."

But the truth was, it wasn't luck. It was law. We knew what was written. And because we knew what was written, we accessed what was rightfully ours.

That moment hit me later as revelation: This is how the kingdom works. Most Christians are standing at the counter of life, getting told, "That doesn't apply to you." They're told the promises of God expired, that favor's only for the spiritual elite, that prosperity's only for preachers on TV.

But the Word says otherwise.

If you don't know what's written, you'll forfeit what's yours. But if you can open the Book, point to the promise, and say, "It is written," everything changes. You move from hoping for favor to standing in it. You stop begging for blessing and start enforcing it.

That's the power of rightly dividing the law.

That's the law of the Word.

# Faith Doesn't Come from Church

Here's the reality that wrecked me: Faith doesn't come from going to church. You can sit in every service, take notes, and "amen" every point. But if you're not hearing the Word for yourself, sowing it, speaking it, and standing on it, you're not actively building faith. You're just spectating.

> So then faith comes by hearing, and hearing by the word of God.
>
> —ROMANS 10:17

That's the formula to actually accessing everything we claim to believe. *Faith comes from hearing the Word*—not opinions, not sermons that barely reference Scripture, not TikTok reels that sound spiritual but aren't rooted in truth, not well-sounding Christian idioms that aren't even scriptural. Faith comes when you hear what God Himself has said and is saying.

I understand it's easier to listen to someone else talk about the Word than to dig in for yourself. But nothing worth having comes easy. You can't live off secondhand revelation or walk in authority with borrowed beliefs. You need the Word in your own spirit, not just in your Instagram's saved folder. Until you start building your faith on the actual Word of God, you'll keep wondering why you're not seeing supernatural results.

Want to build a life of increase? It doesn't start with a thousand-dollar course or a billionaire connection. It starts with the Word. Open it. Hear it. Let it rewire your brain and strip away every excuse and religious mindset you've been taught. The more you hear it, the more you believe it. The more you believe it, the more your life starts to align with what it says.

# You Can't Prosper Past Your Revelation

This explains why some believers stay broke while others step into overflow. It's not ultimately about your love, your effort, or even your giving; *it's about your revelation*. You will never rise above what you believe or prosper beyond what you know. If what you know isn't grounded in God's Word, then what you're building has no foundation.

> My people are destroyed for lack of knowledge.
>
> —HOSEA 4:6

This verse doesn't say the devil destroyed them. It says lack of knowledge did. You can love God and still live in lack if your mind hasn't been renewed by His Word. You can pray in tongues, show up to Bible study, and tithe faithfully while still struggling financially if your belief system is built on tradition instead of truth. God's power flows through revelation of His truth. It doesn't matter what faith target you're aiming at. When you don't know what He said, you're firing a gun full of blanks.

I've lived this reality. Again, I had read the Bible from cover to cover, believed it, and honored it. But there were things around money, increase, and provision that I just couldn't see—not because they weren't in the Word but because I had been taught to explain them away. As a result, I stayed stuck. I was doing all the "right things," but I didn't have the right belief system underneath them. My heart was in it, but my revelation hadn't caught up yet.

When your eyes are opened, when the lights turn on, when you finally see what God has been saying all along, *everything changes.* Your confidence shifts, your language shifts, your giving shifts, and your posture shifts. The results follow because you'll never receive a promise you don't believe, and you'll never believe a promise you haven't seen in the Word for yourself.

## You've Been Lied to About Poverty

This is why so many Christians never step into financial breakthrough: *They've been lied to,* not necessarily by bad people but by bad doctrine. We've already dismantled these lies earlier in the book: that poverty is holy; that wealth is dangerous; that giving without expectation is more spiritual than sowing in faith; that Jesus was poor, and therefore so we should be. We broke that all down scripture by scripture, testimony by testimony, not to hype up prosperity but to dismantle the religious poverty spirit that's robbed the church for generations.

If you've made it this far, you already know that *poverty is not a virtue,* spiritual badge, or proof of your purity. It's a mindset, a system, often resulting from trusting tradition more than truth.

Breaking free from the way you were taught is hard, especially when people you love and respect preached those ideas from pulpits. But just because something was preached by someone you respect doesn't mean it was *biblical*. The only way to expose the lie is to shine the light of the Word on it.

When you start reading Scripture with clear eyes instead of religious filters, you'll realize how much truth has been ignored, skipped over, or explained away. You'll see that Genesis to Revelation is full of covenantal promises. God never hid the principles of financial increase; we just didn't have eyes to see them.

The crazy part? When you point it out, people still push back. They're more comfortable defending lack than learning how to walk in abundance. They say, "Well, I'd rather have Jesus than money," as if those things are mutually exclusive, as if the King who paves His streets with gold is offended if we have some.

The Word tells a different story. The more you open your Bible without fear, bias, or religious tradition twisting your lens, the more you'll see what God *actually* said.

## Read It Without Religion

This was my breakthrough. I had read the Bible from cover to cover multiple times. I wasn't cherry-picking verses or skipping the hard parts. I genuinely loved Scripture and wanted to know what God said. But somehow, I still couldn't see what was right in front of me. I was reading through a lens I didn't even realize I was wearing: the spirit of religion.

Let me clarify what I mean, because *religion* itself isn't the problem. The Bible actually commends true religion: caring for widows and orphans, living purely, walking in integrity (Jas. 1:27). Healthy structure, accountability, and order are gifts from God. The problem isn't organized faith; it's when the organization becomes our god.

The spirit of religion is what the Pharisees carried. It's when we use the rules of God to avoid the heart of God. It's when we honor the text with our lips but ignore the truth with our lives. It's when we're more loyal to denominational tradition than to divine revelation. It replaces relationship with routine, reverence with rigidity, and revelation with repetition.

That's how I was reading the Bible: through filters of fear, loyalty to church culture, and assumptions I'd inherited instead of truths I'd discovered. I wasn't searching for God's intent; I was subconsciously searching for confirmation of what I'd already been told.

Many believers stay stuck there. They're faithful, sincere, and disciplined, but they're feeding on secondhand revelation. They read devotionals and commentaries, they quote sermons, but they rarely open the Word with a clean slate and ask, "Holy Spirit, show me what You meant when You said this."

If you want to break free from lack and walk in supernatural increase, you have to read the Word without that old filter. Take off the lenses of fear and tradition. Let the Holy Spirit—not culture, not commentary, not denominational history—interpret what's written.

When you read without the spirit of religion and let the Word speak plainly, the promises come alive. You stop seeing them as poetic suggestions and start recognizing them as legal guarantees from a covenant-keeping God.

Once you see them, you can believe them. Once you believe them, you can speak them. And once you speak them, you'll start living them.

## Speak What God Said—Not What You See

Once you start reading the Word without religion, the next shift has to happen in your mouth. Believing the Word isn't enough; you have to *speak it*. Just like faith for your salvation works through declaration and confession, so does faith for your increase. You say what God says, even when everything around you says the opposite.

> Death and life are in the power of the tongue, and those who love it will eat its fruit.
>
> —PROVERBS 18:21

Your words are always producing something. Every time you speak, you're sowing seeds into the soil of your future. You're either reinforcing heaven's hope for your life or agreeing with hell's lies. Most Christians don't even realize they're partnering with lack when they flippantly say things like, "I'm broke," "Nothing ever works out for me," or "I can't afford to give right now." Little do they know, they're right—not because it's their prewritten fate but because they're prophesying their own financial ceiling.

When you start speaking the Word, saying what God says instead of what your circumstances say, everything shifts. You're no longer declaring what you see—you're declaring what He promised. That's not delusion; that's faith.

> Now faith is the substance of things hoped for, the evidence of things not seen.
>
> —Hebrews 11:1

Faith doesn't deny what's seen; faith is the evidence of what's not seen. When everything you see is working against you—when your bank account is low, when the clients aren't coming in, when the bills are stacking up—faith isn't ignoring the state you're in. That *is* delusion, not faith. But in the midst of those bad reports, true faith speaks louder. Faith holds the evidence of promises that trump your circumstances. Biblical faith doesn't pretend the problem isn't real; it just refuses to bow down to it.

When you train your mouth to echo only the Word of God, you shut the door on every lie the enemy wants you to believe. You stop partnering with lack, stop speaking death over your future, and start agreeing with what heaven has already declared about you.

You can't live in the promises of God while constantly speaking the opposite. You can't expect prosperity while declaring poverty. If you want to see what God said, you have to start *saying* what God said.

## The Word Doesn't Work Until It's In You

Knowing and speaking the Word is powerful, but until you plant it deep inside you, it won't have the power to produce. Many people hear the Word, quote it, and even post it on social media, but it never gets in them. Until the Word gets in you, it can't produce fruit. The Word is a seed, and like any seed, it doesn't grow until it's planted.

> Your word I have hidden in my heart, that I might not sin against You.
>
> —Psalm 119:11

You have to hide it in your heart—not just memorize it in your head, highlight it in your Bible, or quote it in public. You have to *meditate* on it until it becomes the foundation of your thinking. You need to replace the whisper of lack and doubt that taunts you in the back of your mind with a scripture of victory, hope, and peace. Let the Word sink deep until it starts to shift how you see, how you speak, and how you steward what's in your hands.

If the Word stays surface level, it won't change anything. You'll keep repeating promises that haven't taken root, saying things you don't really believe, getting excited in the moment but frustrated in the waiting. Eventually, you'll think the Word doesn't work, but it does. It always works; *it just doesn't work until it's rooted deep in you.*

Living off verses you heard once isn't enough. You need to meditate on them daily, chew on them, speak them, and plant them so deeply in your spirit that when pressure hits, that's what comes out. Not fear, not doubt, not logic—*the Word.*

When the Word is in you, you stop reacting to circumstances and start responding with truth. You stop needing external motivation and start living from an overflow of internal conviction. You stop chasing break-through and start walking in it.

## The Bible Is the Ultimate Wealth Blueprint

Once the Word is in you, you see it differently. It's not just a devotional book or something to pull out when you need a pick-me-up. It's a reliable blueprint for increase, strategy, generational blessing, and wealth that's built on covenant instead of compromise.

People spend thousands of dollars going to conferences, reading business books, and learning from gurus. I'm not against any of that, but I've found that the most proven, powerful, timeless financial principles I've ever learned weren't in an ebook or a mastermind; they were in Scripture.

Want to know how to prosper? Read Deuteronomy 8; Psalm 112; Proverbs 3, 10, and 11; and Malachi 3. Read what Jesus said in Matthew 6, Luke 6, and Mark 10. Then read 2 Corinthians 9. It's all there, *hidden in plain sight.* He laid out how His kingdom works and showed us what activates blessing, what sustains it, and what disqualifies it.

Most people skip over it. Or worse, they explain it away. They'll say, "Well, that was Old Testament," "That was just for Israel," or "That was spiritual, not literal." But that's not what the Bible says. The Bible doesn't divide itself from itself; deceived people do.

The same God who gave Solomon wisdom to build also gave Joseph the plan to store, gave Abraham the land to own, gave Isaac the hundredfold return, and gave Paul the revelation of cheerful giving. That same God still speaks today, and He speaks through His Word.

If you want to prosper, start treating the Bible like a blueprint. Don't just underline verses; build on them. Don't just highlight promises; apply them. Don't just admire the lives of blessed people in Scripture; emulate their faith.

When you do, you'll stop looking at the Word like it's a religious rule book and start seeing it as the key to everything you've been praying for.

## What You Meditate On You Manifest

Once you start treating the Word like a blueprint, you realize it's not just about what you study; it's about what you meditate on. Meditation isn't passive, empty, or mystical. Biblical meditation is focused repetition, locking in on God's Word until it becomes your reflex.

> This Book of the Law shall not depart from your mouth, but you shall meditate in it day and night....For then you will make your way prosperous, and then you will have good success.
>
> —Joshua 1:8

Want to be prosperous? Want to walk in success? Then meditate on the Word day and night. Speak it, think about it, and obsess over it. Let it shape your perspective more than the news, more than your bank account, and more than your upbringing.

What you meditate on you eventually believe. What you believe you eventually say. What you say you eventually live. This is how the Word becomes flesh in your own life. It doesn't start with discipline; it starts with devotion. You don't need another motivational quote; you need Scripture in your mouth until it changes your mind.

This isn't about once-a-week reflection. I'm talking daily, hourly, again and again. Meditation is not casual but committed, not vague but laser focused on what God said. That's what leads to transformation.

When you meditate on lack, you manifest anxiety. When you meditate on offense, you manifest bitterness. But when you meditate on truth, on promise, on covenant, you manifest the fruit of the Word—not just in your emotions but in your finances, your family, your business, and your purpose.

When you open your Bible with new eyes—without filters, fear, or religion—you'll start to see the truth. God has always been in the business of blessing His people. Prosperity isn't a Western gospel but a covenant promise. He is a rewarder, a multiplier, a provider. He delights in the prosperity of His servant, gives you the power to get wealth, and wants your cup to run over—not so you can brag but so you can bless.

> Let the Lord be magnified, Who takes pleasure in the prosperity of His servant.
>
> —PSALM 35:27, AMPC

> And you shall remember the LORD your God, for it is He who gives you power to get wealth, that He may establish His covenant.
>
> —DEUTERONOMY 8:18

It's all there. The question is, Will you believe it? Will you receive it? Will you meditate on it until it becomes more real than the bills on your desk or the lies you grew up hearing?

This is how the chains break and the cycle ends—not through more hustle but through more revelation. More Word. More truth. More faith. If you want to break poverty, open your Bible.

That's the law of the Word.

## REFLECTION QUESTIONS

1. What scripture about wealth or provision do you need to believe literally instead of symbolically?

2. Where has the world shaped your mindset about money more than the Word has?

3. What promise of increase do you need to start declaring over your business, career, or calling?

Pray this out loud:

*Father, thank You for giving me power through Your Word. As I meditate on Your promises of provision, renew my mind to think like a son or daughter, not a slave. Let every lie about lack be replaced by truth. I receive revelation that prospers me from the inside out. In Jesus' name, amen.*

To access additional resources, scan the QR code or visit thepowertoprosperbook. com/resources.

# THE LAW OF FAITH

**W**HEN REINHARD BONNKE first received a vision from the Lord of a blood-washed Africa, he had no money, no staff, and no platform. Just a word from God and a burden for souls. He began preaching in tents to a handful of people, sometimes so few that the only thing louder than his microphone was his own discouragement. Yet he kept going, kept sowing, kept preaching, not based on what he saw but based on what he believed.

Over time, faith accomplished what effort never could. His ministry expanded from tents to stadiums, from dozens to millions. With seventy-nine million documented salvations, he often said, "I don't want to play with marbles when God told me to move mountains!"[1] His entire life proved one fundamental truth: When you move with faith, heaven moves with you.

This is the law of faith.

## Faith Is the Starting Point of Increase

Faith is not optional. It's not a bonus or something reserved for the "radicals." Faith is the starting point for everything in the kingdom. You can work hard, give generously, quote scriptures, and show up every Sunday. However, if you're not mixing faith into what you do, you won't see supernatural results. Without faith, the Bible says, it's impossible to please God:

> But without faith it is impossible to please Him, for he who comes to God must believe that He is, and that He is a rewarder of those who diligently seek Him.
>
> —HEBREWS 11:6

This verse doesn't just say God is pleased by faith; it declares He *requires* it. You can't even approach Him without it. Faith isn't just belief in God's existence; it's belief in His nature. It's believing that when He says He's a rewarder, He means it. When you seek Him, sow for Him, serve Him, and obey Him, you can confidently expect something in return.

Most people don't truly believe that. They say they do, but they don't act like it. They serve with obligation, give out of fear, and sow out of guilt. Then they wonder why nothing multiplies, why it feels like the Word "isn't working." But the Word does work. The problem isn't with the seed; it's with the expectation.

Look at James 1:6–7:

> But let him ask in faith, with no doubting, for he who doubts is like a wave of the sea driven and tossed by the wind. For let not that man suppose that he will receive anything from the Lord.

If you doubt, don't expect to receive. Sound harsh? That's not my opinion; that's the Word of God. Double-minded people who are half trusting and half panicking shouldn't expect to receive *anything* from the Lord. When we straddle the line of faith with one foot in the camp of "I know God can" but another foot in the camp of "but He probably won't," we just completely handcuff ourselves from seeing the breakthrough we're asking for.

This explains why people stay stuck, give without seeing increase, and serve while remaining empty. They're doing the right things, but they're doing them in unbelief. Unbelief blocks the blessing every single time.

And I'm not saying it's uncommon to struggle with unbelief. We all do. It's part of being human. But just like the father who came to Jesus for his son's healing said, "I believe, but help me in my unbelief," we need to keep our unbelief in check. (See Mark 9:23–26.)

Because when you attach faith to your giving, sowing, and obedience, *the supernatural starts to show up*. Faith is the funnel, the activator that connects your action to the anointing.

## Faith Turns Giving into Worship

So many people miss this. They're giving, but not in faith. Instead of giving with expectation, they do it out of obligation, fear, or pressure, trying to avoid being cursed or to get God off their backs. When they don't see anything happen, they assume the principle doesn't work. But it's not the principle that's broken; it's their posture.

God doesn't just examine *what* you give; He examines *how* you give.

> So let each one give as he purposes in his heart, not grudgingly or of
> necessity; for God loves a cheerful giver.
>
> —2 CORINTHIANS 9:7

God doesn't want reluctant or compulsive giving. He desires joy, freedom, and faith in your giving. A cheerful giver is a believing giver. They're not giving out of fear of what might happen if they *don't*; they're giving in faith for what *will* happen because they did.

This transforms giving into worship. It's not just a transaction; it's a declaration of trust. It's a demonstration of who has your heart and allegiance. It's the awareness that I'm doing this because I believe what God said is true. When He says give and it will be given to you, He means it. When He says the generous soul will prosper, He means it. When He says the measure you use will be measured back to you, He's not teasing you; He's *teaching* you.

People who get excited about giving are usually the ones seeing God move in it because they're not doing it out of religious obligation; they're doing it with worshipful expectation. They know who they're giving to, the ground they're sowing into, and that there's a harvest attached to it.

Rather than giving to check a box, they're giving to honor the One who gave it all, expecting in faith that He will do exactly what He said He would do.

## Faith Is Motivated by Reward

Jesus made it clear: He's not afraid to talk about reward. In fact, He used it to motivate us.

Some people get uncomfortable with this, saying, "Well, I don't serve God for the reward. I just do it because I love Him." While this sounds noble, it's actually unbiblical. God Himself declares He is a rewarder. He didn't say this to manipulate people; He hardwired us to be motivated by reward. It's programmed in our DNA. Expecting God to respond to your obedience isn't fleshly; it's calling Him faithful. Remember, Hebrews 11:6 says God "is a rewarder of those who diligently seek Him."

God wants us to believe that He exists *and* that He rewards. He didn't leave that part out or say, "Believe in Me, but don't expect anything from

Me." He wants us to expect because expectation is what faith *looks* like. Faith isn't passive. Faith doesn't sit in the back row hoping something happens. Faith presses forward, reaches, and moves. Faith *does*.

In fact, Jesus Himself never rebuked people for expecting rewards. He encouraged it, taught it, and celebrated it.

He told us to give and that it will be given to us. He said the measure we use will be measured back to us. He promised that if we give to the poor, we're lending to the Lord, and He will repay us. He said receiving a prophet in the name of a prophet brings a prophet's reward. He told His disciples that even a cup of cold water given in His name won't go unrewarded.

Paul understood this too:

> Run in such a way that you may obtain [the prize].
> —1 CORINTHIANS 9:24

He didn't say run for the sake of running. He said *run to win*. Run with reward in mind, with expectation. Not because you're greedy but because you're obedient to how God designed you.

Jesus loved rewarding faith. Look at the centurion who came to Jesus asking for his servant to be healed. Jesus *marveled*—not because the man was powerful or humble but because he had *faith* (Matt. 8:5–13). The centurion wasn't being presumptuous; he was *expecting* Jesus to move. That expectation moved Jesus.

Consider the woman with the issue of blood. She pushed through the crowd, saying to herself, "If I just touch the hem of His garment, I'll be healed" (Mark 5:28, paraphrased). That wasn't presumption; that was *expectation*. That was faith in action.

Zacchaeus climbed a tree just to get a glimpse of Jesus. That was undignified, desperate faith in action. He believed Jesus would see him. Jesus did, and it changed everything (Luke 19:4–6). When was the last time you chased after the promises of God so desperately you were willing to look like a fool for it?

Throughout the Gospels only two things ever made Jesus *marvel*: faith and the lack of it. Faith moves God. Lack of faith shuts things down. When Jesus returned to His hometown, the Bible says He could not do many mighty works there because of their unbelief (Mark 6:5–6). It was not that He wouldn't; it was that He *couldn't*.

Faith isn't a convenient accessory. It's the access point, the catalyst for your inheritance. When you give in faith, pray in faith, and move in faith, you can expect God to move, too. He's not just the God who sees; He's the God who *rewards*.

## My Giving Changed When I Started Expecting

I used to give out of fear. I tithed faithfully, but I didn't do it with joy or expectation. I did it like paying a spiritual tax. I just didn't want to be cursed or mess up my finances. So I gave cautiously, with hesitation, to check the box. I knew it was the right thing to do, but I didn't know I could expect anything. I didn't realize there was another level of faith I could step into that would actually make giving exciting.

I was hesitant to give to the poor. I wanted to help but felt like I could barely take care of my own family's needs. I wondered, "God, how am I supposed to give to others when I'm already stretched so thin?" But then I started reading the Word, and not just reading it but believing it. I saw what it said about giving, sowing, helping the poor, and the measure being returned. I realized giving wasn't supposed to be a burden; it was supposed to be a breakthrough.

I started putting God's Word to the test. I didn't give recklessly, but I gave *intentionally*. I gave with expectation, in faith rather than fear. That's when everything changed.

I remember when I started giving from my ministry to feed fifty kids a day who wouldn't be able to afford food otherwise. That would've terrified the old me, but I gave in faith. It didn't just feel right; it actually felt fun! I believe God wants to make giving fun again (that would be a cool hat).

Then the testimonies started flowing. I sowed a $2,000 seed into a ministry, and within five days the IRS sent me a $2,500 tax return from three years prior. That was *multiplied* increase. I then sowed another $10,000 seed into that same ministry. Six days later my bank gave me $11,000 back for a mortgage reimbursement. Then I emptied my ministry's bank account—$14,000—and sowed it into another ministry. The next year, God opened up a new stream of income through my ministry and business that brought in about *$140,000*. That's a tenfold return!

Let me be clear: I wasn't giving to manipulate God. I wasn't giving because I thought He owed me something. I was giving because I believed Him. I gave with gratitude, expectation, and vision. I gave because I believed what He said in His Word—that He's a rewarder of those who diligently seek Him, that the measure I use will be measured back to me, and that if I give to the poor, I'm lending to the Lord, and He will repay me.

> He who has pity on the poor lends to the LORD, and He will pay back what he has given.
>
> —PROVERBS 19:17

Is that a metaphor, or is that a promise? When you understand that giving in faith is the ultimate investment strategy, it breaks you out of a poverty mindset. People get excited to invest in crypto, real estate, exchange-traded funds, and business opportunities, but all of those have risk. All of those can fail. But giving into the kingdom? That's a zero-risk investment with an eternal return.

You're not just storing up treasure here; you're storing it in heaven. You're changing lives, advancing the gospel, and doing it in a way that multiplies. There's no safer place to invest than in obedience to God's Word.

When that truth finally sinks in, when giving becomes fun, joyful, and worshipful, you stop hesitating. You start moving in faith.

## The Law of Faith Unlocks the Power of the Word

This is where things really clicked for me. I was hearing the Word, reading the Word, and preaching the Word. But until I started *believing* it, nothing changed. It wasn't that the Word wasn't true or the seed wasn't good. My faith wasn't in it yet. The Word works only when it's mixed with faith.

> For indeed the gospel was preached to us as well as to them; but the word which they heard did not profit them, not being mixed with faith in those who heard it.
>
> —HEBREWS 4:2

That verse right there should shake you because it tells us that *you can hear the Word and still not benefit from it.* You can sit in every Sunday service, read every devotional, and listen to every sermon while still staying stuck. Not because the Word failed but because you never believed it. You heard it, but you didn't mix it, activate it, or move on it.

The Word of God is powerful. It's living, sharp, and full of promise. But without faith it just sits there. Faith is what brings it to life, pulls the harvest out of the seed. When you attach faith to the Word, it starts producing, moving, and multiplying.

This is why I started to see increase, not just because I gave but because I *believed*. I believed God meant what He said. I believed He would reward what I sowed. I believed that when I stepped out, He would step in. That belief turned the Word from information into manifestation.

This separates religious people from faith people. Religious people know Scripture; faith people believe it. Religious people quote it; faith people live it. When you start living *by faith*, you become unstoppable.

## Doubt Disqualifies You from Receiving

Let's get even clearer on how important this warning is. Some people want to talk about blessing and faith but not about what happens when doubt mixes into it. Nobody wants to admit they're struggling to believe God. But if we're going to walk in supernatural provision, we must be honest because the Word is clear: Doubt cancels your harvest. Again, James 1:6–7 says,

> But let him ask in faith, with no doubting, for he who doubts is like a wave of the sea driven and tossed by the wind. For let not that man suppose that he will receive anything from the Lord.

That's not vague or symbolic; that's straight up. If you're double-minded, believing one moment and second-guessing the next, the Bible says you should not expect to receive anything from the Lord. That's a hard word, but it's a good word because it reminds us *resolute faith isn't optional; it's a requirement.*

This explains why some people give and don't see anything. Why some people pray, and nothing moves. It's not that God is holding out on them; they're not standing on His Word. They're treating the promises of God like options instead of guarantees. They're hoping something works, but they're not believing it will. Hope without faith is just wishful thinking.

Doubt is not humility, being careful, or being realistic. It's pride. It's a spiritual liability that decries, "Yeah, I know what God said, *but...*" It calls

God a liar, and then it keeps you in survival mode, paralyzes your obedience, and shuts down the flow of heaven in your life. You can't afford to entertain it. You have to fight it, rebuke it, and replace it with the truth of God's Word—spoken out loud, meditated on day and night, and acted on even when your feelings don't line up.

Faith moves God, but doubt shuts Him out. Again, Jesus didn't do many mighty works in His own hometown because they didn't believe. He *could* and *was willing*, but their doubt disqualified them from receiving.

If we're not careful, the same thing will happen to us. We'll hear the Word, plant seed, and cry out in prayer. But if we're doing it with unbelief in our hearts, we'll walk away empty and blame God for it.

You don't have to live like that. You don't have to settle for a powerless Christian life. Now that you know what doubt can cost you, you can confront it. When you choose faith over fear, belief over doubt, and boldness over hesitation, you'll begin to live like the Word is actually true.

Because it is. When you believe it with everything you've got, you'll see what happens when faith takes over.

## Don't Sow Blind—Sow Believing

Once I realized doubt was costing me, I had a choice to make. I could keep giving just to "do the right thing," or I could start giving with my faith turned all the way on. I could sow like I was planting a tree that might grow one day, or I could sow like I was investing in ground God had already promised to multiply. That shift changed everything for me.

I stopped giving blindly and started giving with eyes to see the future harvest. I began sowing based on the promises of God, not my past experiences of financial stress. I gave to the poor believing God would repay. I sowed into ministries believing God would bring increase. I gave even out of my own lack because I believed the Lord would meet me in it. He did, every single time.

When you believe God's Word, you don't just toss seed into the soil and hope something happens. You sow with confidence, joy, and bold expectation. You don't flinch, hesitate, or second-guess. You believe.

This is what the law of faith is all about. Faith isn't a feeling, theory, or backup plan. Faith is the default position of a believer. It's how we move, speak, give, and receive. If you want to see supernatural provision, to watch God move in ways that don't make sense on paper, and to step into the kind of abundance that overflows into others, you have to stop sowing safe and start sowing in faith.

God's Word is not a gamble; it's a guarantee. When you give like you believe it, live like you believe it, and speak like you believe it, you'll start to see the kind of increase only faith can unlock.

That's the law of faith.

## REFLECTION QUESTIONS

1. In what ways have you been working hard without mixing faith into your work?

2. What financial mountain do you need to start speaking to instead of fearing?

3. How would your giving, building, or investing change if you truly believed God rewards faith?

Pray this out loud:

*Lord, activate supernatural faith within me for finances and purpose. I choose to believe that You are a rewarder. Let faith guide my sowing, planning, and building so that my work produces eternal fruit. In Jesus' name, amen.*

To access additional resources, scan the QR code or visit thepowertoprosperbook.com/resources.

CHAPTER 10

# THE LAW OF OBEDIENCE

THERE'S A TRUE story about an old tightrope walker named Charles Blondin. In the 1800s he became famous for crossing Niagara Falls on a rope. Thousands gathered to watch him perform death-defying stunts, walking blindfolded and even pushing a wheelbarrow across the falls.

One day, after making it safely across, he turned to the crowd and shouted, "Do you believe I can do it again?"

They all roared, "Yes!"

Then he pointed at a man in the front row and said, "Get in the wheelbarrow."

The man froze. He believed in theory, but acting on that belief was entirely different.

That's the difference between admiration and obedience, between agreeing with God's promises and actually living in them. You can believe God is good, say amen to every sermon, and post scriptures on social media. But the real question is, *Will you obey Him?* Will you step into the wheelbarrow when it's your turn? Will you move when He says to, even when it doesn't make sense, costs you comfort, and stretches your faith?

This is the law of obedience.

## Obedience Is Nonnegotiable

Obedience isn't just a good idea in the kingdom; it's nonnegotiable. It's the highway through which every other blessing flows. Recognition of what God has put in your hand isn't enough. Having vision for what it could become isn't enough. Planning the next ten years out perfectly isn't enough. Without obedience, without moving when God says move, everything else stalls.

Obedience is what turns revelation into manifestation.

It's not casual or optional. Jesus said it Himself:

If you love Me, keep My commandments.

—JOHN 14:15

Obedience is not how you receive blessing; it's how you prove your love. It's how you show God, "I trust You more than I trust myself, my feelings, or what I see."

But let's be real. Obedience rarely feels convenient. It seldom fits neatly into our five-year plan and often demands everything we're afraid to lose. It demands surrender of timing, reputation, comfort zones, and outcomes.

## God Responds to Obedience, Not Opportunity

I've walked through this personally more times than I can count. I remember seasons when God asked me to step out in ways that didn't make sense on paper: launching a new ministry when resources were low, building new systems when I was already stretched, hiring people when cash flow said otherwise. Every single time, God honored it. Not because I earned it but because I obeyed.

That's the key: God responds to obedience, not opportunity. He doesn't move because you have a good idea. He moves because you do.

We see this throughout Scripture. Noah didn't wait until the rain started falling to build the ark; he obeyed when there wasn't a cloud in the sky. Abraham didn't wait until Canaan looked affordable; he packed up and moved when God said go. Peter didn't wait until he felt ready to step out of the boat; he obeyed at one word: "Come."

Obedience precedes manifestation. And for many people, God is looking at them the same way He looked at Moses when he was waiting for God to split the Red Sea. He's saying, "Why are you crying to Me? You do it."

## The Cost of True Obedience

Sometimes the obedience God asks for looks ridiculous, reckless, or irresponsible to the natural mind. But that's the tension where faith grows. If obedience were easy, everyone would walk in the anointing. If obedience were convenient, the harvest would be common.

True obedience always costs something, and that's why it's precious to God.

Scripture says,

To obey is better than sacrifice.

—1 SAMUEL 15:22

God isn't impressed by how much you sacrifice on your terms; He's moved by whether you'll surrender on His terms. A sacrifice you control is still about you. Obedience you surrender is all about Him.

I'll be honest. There are moments when obedience will feel like death. Death to your plan, your comfort, your pride. In those moments, everything inside you will want to delay, rationalize, or make a deal with God.

But here's the truth:

- Delayed obedience is disobedience.

- Partial obedience is disobedience.

- Negotiated obedience is disobedience.

God isn't asking for *your version* of His vision for your life. He's looking for people who will move fully, immediately, and joyfully when He speaks.

## The Blessing Is on the Other Side

The truth is, the blessing is on the other side of the obedience.

Sometimes God will ask you to sow a financial seed that stretches you beyond logic. Sometimes He'll ask you to leave a job that feels secure or start something from scratch when the world says you're unqualified. Everything in your flesh will scream that it's too risky.

But if you want to live under the anointing, you have to settle it in your heart: Obedience is never optional.

Obedience positions you for overflow. It moves the hand of God, multiplies the seed, and separates those who talk about faith from those who live by it.

The Word says,

> Blessed are those who hear the word of God and keep it!
>
> —Luke 11:28

There's a blessing attached to hearing, but an even greater blessing attached to doing.

## Living in Radical Obedience

That's the life I want. I don't want to just recognize opportunity, dream big, or make plans. I want to walk in obedience so radical, so quick, so wholehearted, that heaven can't help but move on my behalf.

Because the financial anointing and every other anointing flows not to the talented, not to the popular, not to the well-connected.

It flows to the *obedient*.

That's the law of obedience.

## REFLECTION QUESTIONS

1. What financial or vocational step has God already told you to take, but you've delayed?

2. How has partial obedience limited your increase?

3. What could unlock if you obeyed God completely in this next season?

Pray this out loud:

*Father, align my actions with Your instructions. Give me courage to obey when it costs me comfort. I trust that obedience is the fastest route to overflow and that every act of surrender multiplies my capacity for wealth that serves Your kingdom. In Jesus' name, amen.*

To access additional resources, scan the QR code or visit thepowertoprosperbook.com/resources

## CHAPTER 11

# THE LAW OF RECOGNITION

**D**AD! I HAVE a joke for you!" my seven-year-old son yelled to me from the back of the van. He'd gotten on this kick of making up jokes and trying them on me. Most of them didn't make sense, but I learned to just humor him.

"Let's hear it," I replied, darting my eyes up at the rearview mirror to see him.

"A man was stuck in a hole, and he couldn't get out," my son started. "Then he started to panic! So he prayed to God to give him a ladder, but instead of a ladder, God gave him a tree.

"Then the man yelled, 'I didn't ask for a tree! I asked for a ladder!' So God gave the man a saw. The man yelled again, 'I didn't pray for a saw, God! I prayed for a ladder!' Then God gave the man a hammer and some nails.

"The man yelled one final time, 'God! I'm stuck in this hole, and You're not doing anything to help me! What am I going to do with this tree, this saw, this hammer, and these nails?'

"And then God replied, 'Build a ladder.'"

This is the law of recognition.

## You're Praying for Provision, but You're Holding It

So many people are praying for God to fill their bank accounts, fix their financial crises, or send a miracle check in the mail. God *can* do that— He's still a miracle-working God and the One who provides. But what if the answer to your prayer is already in your hands? What if you're crying out for provision while you're already holding the seed?

That's what Deuteronomy 8:18 says:

> You shall remember the LORD your God, for it is He who gives you power to get wealth, that He may establish His covenant.

Notice it doesn't say God gives you wealth directly. It says He gives *power* to get wealth. That means He gives you the ideas, the gifts, and the raw materials. Your job is to recognize it, activate it, and do something with it.

Most people don't. Most people are begging for a handout when God is trying to make them resourceful. They're asking God to drop checks from heaven when He's saying, "I already gave you the power, the idea, the skill, and the network. You just haven't used it yet."

I walked through this personally during a season when everything was falling apart financially. I was doing the spiritual things: reading the Word, preaching, leading my family. But I wasn't trusting God in this area. I believed He saved me, but I didn't really believe He cared about my financial future.

In that place, I kept praying, "God, meet our needs." Then the Holy Spirit showed me, "You're asking for things I've already made you capable of creating. You're not stuck because I haven't shown up. You're stuck because you haven't recognized what's already in your hand."

Everything started to change in that moment. I stopped asking God for handouts and started asking Him for strategy. I said, "Lord, I don't want You to just give me resources; I want to be *resourceful*." That prayer shifted things. I started looking differently at my gifts, my time, my tools, and the unique anointing on my life. I didn't need more. I needed to see what I already had.

What you've been calling "not enough" might be the very thing God wants to multiply.

## Until You Thank God for It, You Won't See What It Can Do

One of the biggest reasons people don't recognize what's in their hands is they haven't thanked God for it. They're so focused on what they *don't* have, they've lost sight of what they *do*. Here's what I've learned: You will not recognize the miraculous potential in anything that you're not grateful for.

If you won't stop and thank God for it, you'll overlook it, devalue it, and miss the opportunity sitting right in front of you.

Jesus modeled this in John 6 when He fed the five thousand. The disciples were panicking, probably saying, "Lord, send them home! We can't feed all these people!" But Jesus asked them what they had. A little boy stepped forward with five loaves and two fish. It wasn't enough, not in the natural, not in human logic.

But Jesus didn't complain about how small it was. He didn't roll His eyes or send them looking for more. He took what they had and *gave thanks for it*. After He gave thanks, He multiplied it.

That's the pattern: Thanksgiving precedes multiplication. Recognition always comes before increase.

Want to see what God can do with what's in your hands? Start by thanking Him for it. Stop asking for new tools until you've honored the ones He already gave you. Stop wishing you had someone else's platform, skills, or opportunity. Lift your eyes, look at your own life, and say, "God, thank You for what You've already given me. Show me what's hidden in it."

Consider the opposite that happened throughout the wilderness. God delivered Israel out of Egypt, parted the Red Sea, destroyed Pharaoh's army, and literally rained bread down from heaven. But instead of thanking Him for the miracle, the Israelites complained. Instead of saying, "Thank You, God, for feeding us," they said, "Where's the meat?" Instead of honoring the daily provision, they grumbled about the limitations.

What happened? That lack of gratitude cost them their inheritance. That posture of complaint didn't just offend God; it blinded *them*. They couldn't see the Promised Land because they wouldn't even acknowledge the manna.

When you don't thank God for what's in your hands, you go blind to your own provision. You start cursing the very thing that was meant to carry your breakthrough. You start despising the gift that was supposed to lead you into the next level.

God doesn't bless grumbling; He blesses gratitude. Gratitude isn't just about being polite. It's about having eyes to see. It's about having the faith to believe that this little seed, this little start, this little tool or connection or opportunity, could actually be the beginning of something bigger than you imagined.

I've had to do this in my own life repeatedly. There have been seasons when I was tempted to despise what was in front of me, wishing I had more, wishing I had better, wishing I was further along. But every time I brought it before the Lord with gratitude—every time I said, "Thank You for this, Lord, even if it's small, even if it's imperfect"—I started to see the potential in it. I started to get vision for what it could become.

When you thank God, you stop seeing what's in your hands as a leftover and start seeing it as a launchpad. The very thing you've been calling small could be the seed God wants to multiply. But it won't do anything until you recognize it for what it is.

## What Looks Small Is Often the Seed

One of the biggest lies people believe is that they need more to get started. "If I had more time, I'd build something." "If I had more money, I'd invest." "If I had more followers, I'd be faithful with my platform."

But in the kingdom of God you don't wait for overflow in order to begin stewarding. Overflow begins with what's already in your hands. What looks small right now is often not your limitation; it's your seed.

That's what we see in Proverbs 31. This woman is held up as the model of excellence, nobility, and godly productivity. What did she start with? Wool and flax. Two raw materials that, by themselves, don't look like much. But the Bible says she found wool and flax and busily spun it. She didn't despise what she had; she worked it. She saw what it could become. As a result, she didn't just provide for her family, but she enriched her husband's life and brought increase to her entire household.

Proverbs 31:13 says,

> She seeks wool and flax, and willingly works with her hands.

She took what others might have overlooked and turned it into something valuable. That's what recognition looks like. It doesn't wait for a massive door to open. It looks at what God has already given and says, "This is enough to begin."

God's power to make you resourceful is already in your hands. If He's called you to increase, He's already put something in your life that can produce it. Maybe it's a skill, a relationship, an idea, or a resource you've forgotten about or undervalued. But it's there. You're not empty-handed. You just haven't seen it for what it is.

That's how it worked with Moses. When God called him to lead Israel out of Egypt, Moses was full of excuses. "What if they don't believe me? What if I'm not good enough?"

And God said, "What's in your hand?"

It was just a staff. Nothing impressive. But that staff, when surrendered, became the instrument of signs and wonders. It split seas. It silenced pharaohs. It revealed the power of God. All because Moses recognized it. All because he offered it back to the One who gave it.

You don't need the finished product. You need the seed. And the seed is already with you. God didn't make you dependent on someone else's resources to fulfill His call on your life. He's not waiting on you to find the perfect conditions. He's waiting on you to recognize what He already placed in your hand.

Stop calling it small. Stop saying it's not enough. If it came from God, it carries potential. When you sow it—when you work it, spin it, and steward it with faith and vision—it multiplies. But it will never multiply until you stop ignoring it and start honoring it.

Recognition doesn't stop with gratitude. It gets practical. When you start asking the right questions, you begin to unlock the purpose of what's already been given.

## Four Questions That Unlock Recognition

Sometimes the thing in your hands is so close and familiar you don't even notice it anymore. You're praying for God to show you what to build, how to provide, and how to create, and He's saying, "I already gave it to you—you just haven't recognized it yet."

These four questions are simple, but they're powerful. If you answer them honestly, they'll help you uncover the seed God already placed in your life.

### 1. What am I good at?

#### *Focus: your design*

What comes naturally to you that might feel complicated to other people? What do others often ask you to help them with? What do you do well without even thinking about it?

Recognizing what you're good at isn't pride; it's stewardship. You can't multiply what you pretend not to have. If God gave you a skill, He expects you to use it.

## 2. What do I love to do?

### Focus: your desire

Just because you're good at something doesn't mean it energizes you. You might be good at accounting, but it drains the life out of you. So what do you love? What could you spend hours doing without even noticing the time? What makes you come alive?

God doesn't just want you to survive. He wants you to thrive. The thing you love isn't just a hobby; it's a clue. It's part of your design. God often hides direction in your desires.

## 3. What do people need?

### Focus: the world's demand

Recognition moves from internal to external here. We're not here to build something just for ourselves—we're here to serve others. Ask yourself what pain people constantly talk about that you feel a burden to solve. What struggle are you uniquely positioned to help with?

That's where you'll find opportunity. The intersection of your gift and someone else's need is where provision starts to flow.

## 4. What will people pay for?

### Focus: your dominion

This isn't about greed; it's about value creation you can be rewarded for. If you're trying to step into your Deuteronomy 8:18 calling, where God gives you the power to get wealth, then you need to be able to turn your gift into something that can be exchanged. If no one's willing to invest in it, it might be a great idea, but it won't be sustainable.

Don't just chase passion. Find the overlap where your passion solves a real problem, meets a real need, and creates real value. That's where kingdom business is born.

### The overlap is your answer

When you lay those four questions side by side, the overlap is where the recognition happens. That's your seed. That's the resource you've been asking God for. That's your starting point.

Once you recognize what you've been given, the next step is to do something with it.

## You Can't Multiply What You Haven't First Recognized

Too many people ask God to multiply what they haven't even taken the time to notice. They're asking for more but haven't stewarded what's already in their hands. The truth is simple: You can't multiply what you haven't first recognized.

If you're ignoring the thing God already gave you, why would He send something else? God's not going to breathe on what you're unwilling to honor. He's not going to increase what you're unwilling to touch.

Consider the widow in 1 Kings 17. She told the prophet Elijah, "I don't have anything. Just a little flour and a little oil. I was going to make a final meal for myself and my son, and then we were going to die" (v. 12, paraphrased). That's how she saw what she had: insignificant, barely enough, not worth giving.

But Elijah told her, "Make me a small cake from it first" (v. 13). He wasn't being greedy or manipulating her. He was helping her recognize what she already had and helping her put it into the hands of God. When she did, *it never ran out*. The jar didn't empty. The oil didn't stop. What she thought was the end turned out to be the beginning.

You might be looking at what's in your hands right now and thinking, "It's not enough." But what if God sees it differently? What if the thing you've been minimizing is the very key to your overflow? What if the resource you've been overlooking is the one He's been waiting to breathe on, but you haven't brought it to Him yet?

That's what happened to me. There was a season when I felt like I had nothing to work with: no traction, no money, no platform. But I had a camera, and I had a voice. I also had the burden to preach. When I finally stopped asking God to give me something new and started thanking Him for what He already put in my hands, things started to move. I got clarity and direction. I started creating every day. I showed up before anyone was paying attention. And God breathed on it. But it didn't happen until I recognized it.

Deuteronomy 8:18 doesn't say God gives you wealth. It says He gives you the *power* to get wealth: the skill, the idea, the resources, the seed. It's already there. The question is, Do you see it? Do you honor it? Are you working it? Or are you still asking God to bless what you're unwilling to activate?

God doesn't want you dependent on handouts. He wants you to be resourceful. He wants you to multiply what He gave you. But multiplication doesn't start when things get easier. It starts when you recognize what's already in your hands and you work it with gratitude and faith.

Stop asking for more if you haven't taken inventory of what God already placed in your hands. Stop begging for provision when you haven't recognized the seed. God's not holding out on you. He's waiting for you to open your eyes. He's waiting for you to stop despising small beginnings and start thanking Him for the raw materials.

What looks like wool and flax to everyone else might be the beginning of your breakthrough. What looks like just five loaves and two fish might be the start of a supernatural overflow. What looks like just a staff in your hand might be the thing God uses to split the sea.

But it all begins with this: recognizing what He already gave you, giving thanks for it, and moving in faith.

That's the law of recognition.

## REFLECTION QUESTIONS

1. What resource, relationship, or idea has God already placed in your hand to create value?

2. How could gratitude reveal hidden opportunities for increase?

3. What overlooked skill could become a stream of income if you worked it with faith?

Pray this out loud:

*God, open my eyes to see the seeds of prosperity already in my possession. Thank You for the tools, gifts, and ideas You've entrusted to me. Teach me to honor them, develop them, and multiply them for Your glory and for the advancement of Your kingdom. In Jesus' name, amen.*

To access additional resources, scan the QR code or visit thepowertoprosperbook.com/resources.

## CHAPTER 12

# THE LAW OF VISION

**T**HERE'S AN OLD story about Walt Disney that has always stayed with me. When Disney World was finally completed in Florida years after Walt's death, someone at the grand opening leaned over to his widow and said, "It's a shame Walt didn't live to see this."

She looked back and replied, "He did see it. That's why it's here."

Vision always comes first. Before the buildings. Before the systems. Before the harvest. First comes a vision that others can't see yet, and then comes the fruit everyone can't help but notice. That's the power of vision, and that's the next biblical law that accelerates the financial anointing: the law of vision.

## Vision Always Comes First

Before you can prosper, before you can plan, before you can even recognize what's in your hands, *you need vision*. You need to see beyond where you are. You need to believe there's something on the other side of your current circumstance that's worth working toward.

That's what vision does. It pulls you forward. It tells you that what you're doing today matters for where you're going tomorrow. It helps you wake up early, stay focused, and endure long seasons when it feels like no one is watching. Without vision even the most anointed gift will go unused because vision is what gives direction to your diligence.

The Bible says in Proverbs 29:18,

> Where there is no revelation, the people cast off restraint.

Without vision people throw off discipline. They give up on order. They live in reaction mode. And I've seen this, especially in areas of poverty or generational brokenness. If you grow up in an environment where no one's thinking past tomorrow, where all you see is dysfunction, where there's no blueprint for progress, then vision becomes the first miracle.

Because consequences mean nothing to people without vision. They'll blow up their marriages, throw away jobs, gamble their futures—because in their minds there was never anything to protect in the first place. That's the power of vision. It creates restraint. It creates purpose. It gives weight to your yes and clarity to your no.

If you don't get vision first, nothing else will stick. You'll fall back into the same patterns. You'll procrastinate, self-sabotage, and talk yourself out of building what God told you to build. Not because you don't want it but because you can't *see* it. That's why vision has to come before everything else. Before you make a plan. Before you build a business. Before you try to scale your ministry. If you don't see it clearly in your spirit, you won't carry it consistently in the natural.

This is something I've had to walk through myself. The hardest mornings to get out of bed are the ones when I lose sight of where I'm going. When I'm thinking about today in isolation—just trying to survive the next to-do list, just trying to make it through—everything feels heavy.

But when I'm locked into the vision, when I see where God is taking me, when I see how it connects to my family, my team, the people I'm called to reach, and the fruit I'm called to bear, that's when it becomes easy to show up. That's when work becomes worship. That's when planning becomes joy. Because I'm not just reacting. I'm building.

You can't steward what you haven't seen. You can't multiply what you haven't envisioned. That's why so many people stay stuck, not because they're lazy but because they're blind. They're waiting for something to change externally when what they really need is vision internally.

When that vision clicks in place, everything else aligns. Suddenly, the things that felt like sacrifices start to feel like investments. Suddenly, the seasons that felt hidden start to feel holy. Because now you know what you're moving toward.

## Vision Builds Restraint

When you don't have vision, you start casting off restraint. You just do whatever you want. You don't think about the ramifications because you're not seeing past the moment. That's what happens in places marked by brokenness. That's why you see entire regions stuck in generational poverty, not just because of economics but because there's no vision. There's a very poor area in Omaha, Nebraska, the city where I pastor, and one of my pastoral friends has an incredible quote that reflects his compassion for this underserved part of our community. He says, "To those without hope, consequences mean nothing." When people don't see what's possible, they can't imagine a future beyond survival.

When you don't have vision for something better, you just live for the now. You don't build. You don't prepare. You don't protect what you're carrying.

But when you do have vision—when you've seen what could be, when you've caught a glimpse of the promise—it changes everything. It puts boundaries around your life. It makes you selective. It helps you endure.

Vision is what keeps you from quitting. It's what gives you endurance when things get hard. It's what reminds you, "This sacrifice matters because of where I'm going."

Consequences mean nothing to people without vision. That's why some people blow their shot. They'll destroy their marriage, they'll gamble their future, they'll walk away from God-ordained assignments—*not* because they're evil but because they have no picture of what they're giving up. They have no awareness of what could have been.

Vision keeps you anchored. Vision gives you something to protect. It helps you make wise decisions, not just based on today but based on the future you're building toward.

I believe that's what God wants to restore to a lot of people right now. The enemy has tried to beat the vision out of you. He's tried to bury it under distraction, discouragement, and past disappointments. But vision is how you fight back. Vision is how you keep moving. Vision is how you build a future that outlasts what you're currently walking through.

## Vision Doesn't Just Serve You— It Builds for Others

When God gives you a vision, it's never just about you. It's always about what He wants to do *through* you. It's about the people you're called to reach, the systems you're called to build, the lives that are supposed to be blessed because of your obedience.

That's what legacy vision looks like. It's not just asking, "How do I make my life easier?" It's, "How do I build something that makes life better for others?" That's the difference between ambition and assignment. Ambition stops with comfort. Vision multiplies into calling.

That's what you see with Nehemiah. He wasn't a pastor. He wasn't a prophet. He was a cupbearer. But when he heard the walls of Jerusalem were in ruins, it broke his heart. He had a vision of what it could've been.

He didn't sit around and pray that someone else would do something. He asked the king for permission and provision to rebuild. And when the king said yes, Nehemiah didn't just run on passion; he ran on vision. He planned, organized, and rallied people. And brick by brick, they rebuilt the wall.

That's what happens when vision becomes generational. You don't just think about how to get by; you start thinking about how to restore and multiply, how to leave behind something that outlives you.

This is what Proverbs 13:22 is all about: "A good man leaves an inheritance to his children's children." That's vision! That's what happens when you stop asking, "How do I get ahead?" and start asking, "How do I build something that lasts?"

That's the kind of vision God wants to give you. Not just a vision for success. A vision for legacy. A vision that blesses your family. A vision that opens doors for others. A vision that provides for your children's children. A vision that outlasts your job title, your platform, your phase of life.

That's the kind of vision God honors. That's the kind of vision that attracts heaven's backing.

Vision is the starting point of everything. Without it you'll cast off restraint. Without it you'll waste your effort, your energy, and your potential, chasing distractions that look urgent but aren't eternal.

When you carry vision from God, when you see what He sees, it changes how you live. It builds endurance into your obedience. It brings meaning to your sacrifice. It lifts your eyes from surviving the moment to building for generations. And it reminds you that this isn't just about you. It's about who will be impacted by your yes.

So ask Him for vision. Receive it with gratitude. Guard it with your life, and then move toward it with conviction. Because what you see in your spirit will eventually shape what you see in your world. And when that vision becomes realized, it commands tremendous financial reward.

That's the law of vision.

# REFLECTION QUESTIONS

1. What picture of prosperity has God shown you that you've been afraid to pursue?

2. How does your personal vision connect to advancing God's kingdom on earth?

3. What disciplines will keep your financial vision clear when distractions arise?

Pray this out loud:

*Lord, expand my vision beyond survival. Let me see wealth the way You do—resources serving redemption. Give me heavenly imagination to build businesses, ministries, and systems that reflect Your abundance and fund Your mission. In Jesus' name, amen.*

To access additional resources, scan the QR code or visit thepowertoprosperbook. com/resources.

# CHAPTER 13

# THE LAW OF PLANNING

**I**N 1912 THE *Titanic* set sail with elegance, confidence, and more luxury than the world had ever seen. It was considered the crown jewel of engineering: a ship so advanced that newspapers called it unsinkable. But only four days into its maiden voyage, it struck an iceberg in the northern Atlantic and sank to the bottom of the ocean. More than 1,500 people lost their lives.

What most people don't realize is that the *Titanic* had lifeboats for only about half of its passengers, not because there wasn't room for more but because the planners believed they'd never be needed. They were so confident in the strength of the ship that they failed to prepare for the possibility of a storm.

It wasn't the iceberg that doomed them; it was the arrogance of assuming they couldn't fail. They had vision, but they didn't have preparation.

The same thing happens in business, ministry, and finances today. People dream big, talk big, even believe big—but they don't build for adversity. They speak faith but never create systems. They pray for growth but never plan for it. Then when the storm comes, what they built sinks—not because God wasn't faithful but because they weren't prepared.

That's the difference between vision and stewardship—between what you hope happens and what you prepare for. And that brings us to the next law that accelerates the financial anointing: the law of planning.

## God Doesn't Bless Disarray— He Blesses Preparedness

There's a false idea floating around in Christian culture, especially in ministry, that planning is somehow "less spiritual." That if you have an order to your service, know your message points, or prepare your strategy, you're not leaving room for the Holy Spirit. I've been doing ministry for a long time now, and I can tell you this mindset is keeping people stuck. That's not how God operates or what Scripture teaches. God is not intimidated by your planning. In fact, He expects it.

The Bible literally says in Hebrews 9:1,

> Then indeed, even the first covenant had ordinances of divine service and the earthly sanctuary.

The old covenant, filled with sacrifices, offerings, feasts, and laws, had divine ordinances. That means structure, systems, and a spiritual plan. When God gave instructions to Moses for the tabernacle, He gave blueprints, measurements, materials, and order. He didn't say, "Just feel it out." He gave specifics because God works through order. Yet somehow, we've developed this idea that the less prepared we are, the more Spirit led we must be. But that's not spiritual; it's sloppy.

We say we want revival, but we don't have any structure to carry it. We say we want overflow, but we haven't even created the container for the overflow to land in. God doesn't pour into chaos. He multiplies what's been yielded to Him and prepared for Him. If your life is in disarray, if your systems are constantly playing catch-up, if you're always scrambling at the last minute and expecting God to bless it, don't call that faith. That's presumption.

A man prepares his way, but the Lord directs his steps. That means planning is *your* responsibility, and direction is *His*. Too many people are waiting on direction, with nothing built underneath it, and then they wonder why nothing is moving forward. Planning is how you make room for movement. You may not have all the answers or know every step, but if you haven't made the effort to map out what you do know, how do you expect God to multiply it?

Planning is spiritual, is powerful, and shows God you're serious. When you take what He's given you and put it into structure, you're not boxing Him in—you're inviting Him in. You're saying, "God, I believe You want to do something through this, so I'm going to build like You will." If you're not building in faith, then you're just winging it in fear. And that's not what God honors.

This is why we need to talk about the false tension people feel between planning and being Spirit led. Because those two things are not enemies; they were always meant to go together.

## The Holy Spirit Is Not Allergic to Order

What is with this strange tension in the church that makes people think planning is somehow unspiritual? Like if you map something out, it means you're not being led by the Spirit. But I want to speak directly to that mindset: The Holy Spirit is not allergic to order. He's not put off by structure or intimidated by spreadsheets. He doesn't leave when someone opens their calendar. If anything, He shows up when He sees someone has made room for Him to move.

Again, that's what Hebrews 9:1 shows us. There were divine ordinances, systems, regulations, and preplanned instructions for stewarding the presence of God. The tabernacle didn't just appear out of nothing or evolve from the sand; it was designed with intention and built with precision. God gave every single detail. So if you're saying the Holy Spirit can show up only in chaos, that's not biblical. That's just your preference dressed up in false spirituality.

I've heard the criticism before. "This church is too structured. It's too programmed. I just want the Holy Spirit to move." I get where people are coming from. They're hungry for the supernatural and don't want God to feel scripted. But here's the truth that rarely gets preached: Spontaneity is not the only evidence of the Spirit. Sometimes the most Spirit-filled move you can make is to plan something in advance under His direction and then execute it in obedience.

But let's go further. What if the Holy Spirit was present when the plan was made? What if He was the One who gave the wisdom, strategy, and structure? We act like planning and Spirit-led living are on opposite ends of the spectrum, but they were always meant to go hand in hand. The Bible says a man plans his way, but the Lord directs his steps (Prov. 16:9). It doesn't say he waits around for steps to be handed to him. It says he *plans*. That's your part. When you do that part with God in humility and dependence, He will direct what you've built.

Too often people overly spiritualize chaos. They treat their lack of preparation like it's a virtue. "I didn't prepare anything; I'm just letting the Spirit lead." But if you never prepared, how do you know the Spirit wasn't leading you *before* you stepped on the stage? How do you know He didn't want to give you wisdom in the quiet place so you could lead with clarity in the public one? The biblical pattern shows that God moves in order. From Genesis to Revelation we see it again and again. He speaks into chaos and brings form. He takes disorder and creates function. That's the Spirit's rhythm.

Planning doesn't box God in. It reflects His character. It acknowledges that what He's entrusted to you matters. When you take the time to map things out—not just for ministry but for your finances, family, and business—you're not stepping away from the Spirit. You're demonstrating that you trust Him enough to steward well what He gave you.

## Vision Without Planning Is Just Presumption

So let's connect this with your vision for financial increase. You can have the clearest vision in the world, but if you don't have a plan for it, it's not going to go anywhere. And that's not a faith problem; it's a planning problem. There are so many believers walking around frustrated because they feel like God gave them a vision but nothing's happening. It's not because God lied or the vision wasn't real. It's because they never built a system to carry what they asked God for. That's what happens when you confuse vision with strategy. Vision gives you direction, but without planning it turns into presumption.

You can't just say, "I'm trusting God," and do nothing to prepare. That's not trust. That's laziness dressed up in Christianese. Proverbs 24:27 (NLT) says,

Do your planning and prepare your fields before building your house.

Before you start building, you prepare the field. You lay the groundwork and get the soil ready. You don't just say, "God gave me a word," and start hammering nails into a foundation that doesn't exist yet. You make a plan. You ask the Holy Spirit to give you strategy. You think long-term and write it out in detail because faith doesn't cancel structure—*faith demands it.*

I had to learn this personally. In my own ministry I was praying for growth, asking God for favor, reach, and resources. But at the same time I was barely planning my live streams and preparing teachings week to week, scrambling just to show up. I started realizing I was asking God to increase something I hadn't built to sustain growth. That's when I felt the Lord impress this question on my heart: "Why would I bless what you haven't prepared for?" That hit me. If I really believed God wanted to do something big through my ministry, why wasn't I creating a structure that could handle the weight of it? This took me to another level of rigorous preparation in my live stream outlines, my video editing processes, my marketing funnels and automations, my pipelines for serving the lives God was sending us, and our donation reception processes.

You may be in that same place. You've been praying for increase, but God is waiting to see if you'll get serious about the infrastructure. He's waiting to see if you'll actually build the system. If He sent the rain today, it would flood and wash everything out. Planning is how you build the irrigation before the rain. Planning is how you show God you're not just daydreaming; you're partnering with Him to make the vision real.

There are people asking God for a seven-figure business, but they don't have a sales plan. People are asking God to grow their YouTube channels, but they haven't mapped out their content calendars. People are praying for staff, but they don't have systems in place for onboarding or leadership. It's not that the desire is wrong. There's just no plan! The gap between vision and execution is filled with intentional planning.

You're not waiting on God to move. He's waiting on you to plan.

## Make Room for What You're Praying For

There are a lot of people praying big prayers. They're asking God for abundance, multiplication, and overflow. God's not offended by that. He wants to bless, increase, and entrust more. But He's looking for people who will actually make room for what they're asking Him for. That's what planning really is: *making room.*

You can't keep praying for God to expand your business if you're still running everything out of your head. You can't keep asking for new clients if you haven't mapped out your onboarding process. You can't keep asking God to bless your finances if you don't even know where your money is going. And you can't expect favor to fall if you haven't created the capacity to carry it.

Planning isn't about controlling every variable. It's about stewarding what's in your hands and trusting God with the part that's not. I remember when I hit a point where I realized I needed to start planning my teachings better. I was going live every week just trying to pull something together. But God had given me a vision and shown me what was possible. Yet I was treating it casually. I was showing up without structure and hoping God would fill in the gaps. The truth was, I hadn't built a system for favor to rest on.

That was a turning point for me. Once I started treating the vision like it mattered, planning with intention, things shifted. I wasn't scrambling or guessing. I had clarity, direction, and room for God to move. That's what planning does. It makes room for miracles. It creates space for what God wants to send. It says, "I'm not just hoping You'll move; I'm ready when You do."

So wherever you are right now, I want you to ask yourself these questions honestly: Have I made room for what I've been praying for? Have I built the structure? Have I mapped the systems? Have I taken inventory of what God's already given me? Have I prepared the field? Because if not, that's your next step. Not another fast, not another seed, not another prophetic word. Build the plan. Make it plain. And then move on it.

Because God is not waiting for you to be perfect. He's waiting for you to be prepared.

So many people are crying out for more—asking God to open doors, send opportunity, and release overflow. And God is willing. But He's also wise. He doesn't pour into chaos; He pours into structure. He doesn't multiply confusion; He multiplies stewardship. Until you get serious about planning, about writing the vision, preparing the field, and building something that can actually hold what you're asking for, you'll keep living in cycles of frustration. God doesn't bless disorder. He blesses what's been surrendered and prepared. So make the plan. Map it out. Create a structure that faith can fill. Because when you do, you're not just organizing your life; you're making room for the miraculous.

That's the law of planning.

# REFLECTION QUESTIONS

1. Where do you need to create structure so God can trust you with more?

2. How could better planning turn your calling into a sustainable enterprise?

3. What plan could you write today that would prove you're expecting increase?

Pray this out loud:

*Father, give me wisdom to organize the blessing. Help me steward opportunities with excellence and build structures worthy of Your trust. I prepare not from fear but from faith that You will fill what I build. In Jesus' name, amen.*

To access additional resources, scan the QR code or visit thepowertoprosperbook.com/resources.

## CHAPTER 14

# THE LAW OF DILIGENCE

WHEN THOMAS EDISON was trying to invent the electric light bulb, he didn't just have one idea and hope it worked. He tested over a thousand different materials. Filament after filament, experiment after experiment, failure after failure. Yet every time one failed, he didn't call it wasted; he called it data. When asked how it felt to fail a thousand times, he said, "I have not failed. I've just found 10,000 ways that won't work."[1] That kind of perseverance changed history. The world didn't reward his brilliance; it rewarded his diligence. Innovation wasn't the result of inspiration alone but the result of consistency, of showing up, of refusing to quit.

This is the law of diligence.

## God Doesn't Bless Stagnation— He Honors Movement

God does not bless laziness. He doesn't bless passivity or the person who sits around folding their hands, waiting for a miracle to drop out of the sky. The Bible says in Proverbs that the lazy man desires and has nothing, but the hand of the diligent will prosper (Prov. 13:4). God honors movement. He honors people willing to put their hand to the plow and work what He's already given them, even when they're not seeing immediate results. The blessing doesn't fall on wishful thinking—it falls on obedient action.

There's a popular Christian idea that sounds spiritual but keeps people stuck: "I'm just waiting on God." Often, the truth is that God is waiting on *you*. He's waiting to see what you'll do with what He already gave you, waiting to see if you'll put your hand to the seed, to the vision, to the opportunity. If you won't work what He's already placed in your hand, why would He trust you with more?

Proverbs 6:10–11 doesn't mince words about this:

A little sleep, a little slumber, a little folding of the hands to sleep—so shall your poverty come on you like a prowler, and your need like an armed man.

There's danger in putting things off, in passivity. Poverty doesn't always hit because of bad breaks; it often hits because of delayed action. You think you have more time, that tomorrow is when you'll get serious. But the Word says poverty comes like a thief in the night: subtle, then sudden.

Consider Ruth's example. She was widowed with nothing: no money, no title, no future. When opportunity came, she didn't sit around waiting for someone to fix her life. She got to work, went into the fields, and gleaned behind the harvesters. She worked with diligence and humility, catching Boaz's attention. Her diligence didn't just feed her; it positioned her for generational legacy. She went from gleaning scraps to becoming the great-grandmother of King David. That's what God does with diligence: He takes what looks like grinding and turns it into glory.

I've seen it repeatedly: people who say they're believing for breakthrough but are living in spiritual inertia. They listen to sermons all day but do nothing with their hands, consuming content and calling it growth. But if you're not doing the work, you're not going to see the reward. Faith without works is dead. And in the same way, vision without diligence is fantasy.

Being diligent doesn't always feel spiritual, especially when it's behind the scenes and no one's noticing. But even if people don't see it, *God does*. Every time you show up early, honor your commitments, or give your best when it would be easier to coast, God is taking notice. He's not just watching for the big, flashy moments; He's watching how you manage the small, the quiet, the mundane.

God can't multiply what you won't move on. Favor doesn't fall on stagnation; it falls on stewardship. You can ask God for blessing, but if you're not putting your hand to anything, what exactly is He supposed to bless? Some people are stuck not because the enemy is attacking but because they're not moving. They're waiting for breakthrough but haven't done anything to build a foundation for it.

Go to the ant, O sluggard; consider her ways, and be wise....She prepares her bread in summer and gathers her food in harvest.

—PROVERBS 6:6–8, ESV

That's what diligence looks like: quiet, consistent, strategic. She's not praying for harvest when it's time to reap; she's already storing it up. She's not scrambling in winter because she put the work in when the sun was shining. That's the posture God honors, the posture the enemy fears.

## Diligence Is the Weapon the Devil Fears

If there's one thing the enemy fears more than your gifting, it's your consistency. He's not threatened by your passion in a single moment; he's threatened by your refusal to quit when no one's clapping. That's why one of the devil's favorite strategies isn't just temptation; it's exhaustion. If he can't make you fall, he'll try to make you stop.

Galatians 6:9 addresses this directly:

> Let us not grow weary while doing good, for in due season we shall reap if we do not lose heart.

Notice it doesn't say, "You'll reap because you're gifted." It says you'll reap if you don't quit. Diligence is spiritual warfare. Every day that you show up and sow when no one sees it, hell trembles. Every time you record another video, write another post, serve another person, or clean up something no one thanked you for, you're warring against the lie that your obedience doesn't matter. The devil wants you to think it's pointless so you'll stop short of your harvest. But Scripture is clear: In due season, you will reap.

I've seen it firsthand. There are people who have more natural talent, more resources, more connections, but they don't have endurance. They don't keep digging or showing up. Because of that, they miss out on what God wanted to give them—not because they were disqualified but because they disqualified themselves by giving up too soon. Diligence is how you guard your destiny and steward the ground you've been assigned.

Think about Joseph in the Old Testament. He wasn't promoted because he had a dream. He was promoted because he worked with diligence everywhere he was placed. As a slave he prospered. As a prisoner he was elevated. Why? Because he kept showing up. He didn't wait until he was in the palace to carry excellence; he carried it in the pit, in chains, in obscurity.

When God opened the door to Pharaoh's court, Joseph didn't step into his breakthrough unprepared; he was ready.

That's what diligence does. It keeps you sharp in hidden seasons, builds muscle when no one's watching. When the opportunity finally comes (and it *will* come), you'll be able to step into it without flinching because you'll have already been doing the work in private.

Don't let the devil lie to you. Don't let him convince you that your labor is wasted, your effort ignored, your obedience meaningless. He wants you to quit and burn out. But if you stay planted and faithful, you *will* reap.

## Consistency Is How You Outpace Talent

We live in a world that celebrates giftedness, but God honors consistency. Talent may get you noticed, but diligence is what makes you unshakable. You don't need to be the most charismatic or have the most impressive résumé. You don't even need to be the best in the room. You just have to refuse to quit.

According to Proverbs 13:4,

> The soul of a lazy man desires, and has nothing; but the soul of the diligent shall be made rich.

That's the difference. The lazy person has desire, vision, dreams—but nothing ever comes of it because they never do anything with it. The diligent, on the other hand, may not be flashy, but they move. They act, execute, and do the work no one sees. Eventually, they carry a reward everyone notices.

Consistency is a cheat code in the kingdom. The people who make the biggest impact aren't always the most brilliant; they're just the ones who didn't give up. They showed up when they were tired, created when they didn't feel inspired, and stayed faithful to what God put in front of them even when it didn't seem to be producing fruit. Over time, *that diligence compounds.* That's how God works: He honors the ones who keep going.

You can't control how talented someone else is, but you can control how consistent you are. You can't make favor fall on your timeline, but you can make sure you're still in position when favor shows up. The problem is, too many people are looking for shortcuts. They want hacks, a harvest without a process. But kingdom success is slow: It's planted, watered, cultivated. Then, *after a while*, it starts to grow.

If you feel overlooked, if you feel like your effort isn't making a difference, don't quit. Don't back down or get casual. In a culture full of people who start and stop, who get hyped and then burn out, your consistency will outlast them all.

## Diligence in the Dark Produces Fruit in the Light

Building my YouTube channel taught me the power of hidden seasons. For the first several months, I was creating content in complete obscurity. My basement studio had no fancy lighting, no professional setup—just me, a camera, and an unshakable belief that God had called me to this. Day after day, I recorded messages that felt like they were disappearing into a void. The view counts were small, the comments were few, but I kept sowing. I was posting multiple videos daily, not because I saw immediate results but because I trusted the process. Then suddenly, everything shifted. What had been slow, steady growth exploded overnight.

The channel went from ten thousand to one hundred thousand subscribers in less than a month. But that overnight success was actually the fruit of months of faithful work in the dark. The breakthrough didn't happen because I finally got good—it happened because God honored the seeds I'd been planting when no one was watching.

That's what diligence does. It produces fruit in the light because it was faithful in the dark.

Ecclesiastes 11:6 (NIV) puts it this way:

> Sow your seed in the morning, and at evening let your hands not be idle, for you do not know which will succeed, whether this or that, or whether both will do equally well.

You don't always know which seed will be the one God breathes on. You don't get to pick the video that goes viral or the message that hits just right. But you do get to show up, sow, and be found working. The only people who don't see a harvest are the ones who stop sowing too soon. God is not mocked—what a man sows he will also reap. But you can't reap what you didn't plant.

There are many people asking God to bless them publicly, but they haven't been willing to grind privately. They want platform without process, promotion without hidden obedience. But God promotes those who steward well in secret. Joseph didn't get handed Pharaoh's palace out of nowhere. He was diligent in Potiphar's house and in prison. Then in a moment, everything shifted. But it wasn't sudden to God; it was the reward of years of hidden faithfulness.

Don't despise your hidden season or waste your obscurity. Don't rush the process just because no one's clapping. You're not working for man—you're working unto the Lord. He sees the seed, the effort, every early morning and late night. When the time is right, He will make it visible. For now, just keep digging, posting, and showing up.

The ones who will shine later are the ones who sowed consistently when no one else was paying attention.

## Excellence Is Not Optional—It's Expected

One of the things that frustrates me most about the state of Christianity is the complete lack of excellence I see in so many areas. Somewhere along the way, we decided that spiritual sincerity is enough and that diligence doesn't matter. We act like showing up late doesn't matter, doing the job halfway doesn't matter, and sloppiness can somehow be spiritual. Let me say this as clearly as I can: God is not glorified by sloppiness. He is glorified by stewardship.

There are believers wondering why they're not getting promoted, why their businesses are plateauing, why their ministries aren't gaining traction. The truth is, it's not always the devil holding them back—it's the fact that they're not showing up with excellence. They're submitting sloppy work, emailing clients or church members with typos and no formatting, walking into the office unprepared, showing up late, not dressing appropriately, and not following through. Then they wonder why favor isn't following them. If you're not willing to do the small things with care, why would God trust you with more?

Even from an employer's perspective, think about it: If you're in a position to hire or promote someone, are you going to give more responsibility to the person who can't even get the basics right? No. You're going to invest in the one who's paying attention, who's thoughtful, who's taking seriously what they've been given. That's not legalism; that's common sense. If that's how we function in the natural, how much more would God, who sees everything, respond to those who carry themselves with intentionality and honor?

Diligence is evangelism. It tells the world who your God is. When people see how you show up—how you speak, finish your tasks, lead your teams—they get a picture of who you belong to. You might give the only sermon they ever read. If your work ethic is chaotic, your life messy, and your communication lazy, what message does that send? What does it tell people about the God you serve?

This isn't about being perfect or striving; it's about understanding that how you carry yourself *matters*. Your diligence is a witness; your preparation is a testimony. When you do things with care, intentionality, and consistency, you don't just represent yourself—you represent the kingdom.

Don't treat excellence like it's optional or treat the little things like they're beneath you. In the kingdom the little things are the test. If you can be found faithful there, God will elevate you in ways you couldn't orchestrate on your own.

## Diligence Is the Setup for the Transfer of Wealth

I believe with all my heart that we are in a very unique window right now: a prophetic moment. There is a transfer of wealth coming, a shift from the hands of the unrighteous into the hands of the righteous. But it's not going to everyone—it's going to the *diligent*, the ones who are working the land God gave them, applying His laws, building His systems, and showing Him they're serious.

We're in a moment when the economy feels unstable. People are worried about inflation, recession, the political landscape, tariffs, and trade wars—all the things that make headlines. Those things matter, but this is not the time to shrink back or get lazy and fearful. This is the time to *work*, to press in, to build with God. The ones who do this season right will reap something in the next season that can't be explained by natural conditions.

I'm not saying this to hype you up. I'm saying it because I've seen it and lived it, and I'm watching it happen right now. There are people who will come out of this season with things they never imagined, not because they chased opportunity but because they were diligent with what God already gave them. The favor that's coming isn't random; it's for those who are found *faithful*.

Make no mistake. This transfer of wealth is not about selfish gain, showing off, or collecting things to impress people. This is about *kingdom assignment*. God is looking for people willing to be funnels, not buckets—people who will take what He pours out and put it to use for His glory, people who will think generationally, fund the harvest, disciple nations, raise up leaders, and build infrastructure that points to Jesus.

If you want to be trusted with that kind of resource, you need to be diligent now. Not later, not when the door opens—*now*. You need to steward your assignments with excellence, take your schedule seriously, and treat what's in your hands like it matters, because it does.

If you're praying for breakthrough, believing for expansion, asking God to bless your business, your ministry, your vision—start with diligence. Start by honoring what's already in front of you. God is watching, and He's not just looking for those who can dream big; He's looking for those who can carry the weight of what they're asking for.

When He finds someone diligent, He doesn't just reward them with increase; He trusts them with legacy.

Wherever you are, whatever God's put in your hands—work it with everything you've got. What you're doing now is not just building provision; it's building trust, capacity, and something God can multiply.

That's the law of diligence.

# REFLECTION QUESTIONS

1. What assignment have you left half done that could produce fruit if finished?

2. How is consistency the missing key between your seed and your harvest?

3. Where do you need to upgrade your work ethic to match your level of faith?

Pray this out loud:

*God, anoint my hands for diligence. Strengthen my focus, remove laziness, and fill my labor with joy. Help me show up every day as a faithful steward of the power You've given me to create wealth. In Jesus' name, amen.*

To access additional resources, scan the QR code or visit thepowertoprosperbook.com/resources.

CHAPTER 15

# THE LAW OF CHARACTER

THERE'S A POWERFUL story about Ulysses S. Grant, the American Civil War general who later became president of the United States. Early in his military career, Grant faced severe hardship. He was wrongfully accused of misconduct and pressured into resigning his post. Most men would have quit altogether, retreated into bitterness, tried to cut corners, or compromised to regain power. Grant didn't. He humbled himself; worked small, unnoticed jobs; and kept his integrity intact. When the Civil War broke out years later, America needed a leader it could trust. Grant's private character, tested in anonymity, made him the man who would eventually lead a nation to victory.

Character doesn't always pay immediately, but it always pays ultimately. That's why the next law that accelerates financial anointing is the law of character.

## Character Is the Foundation for Promotion

You can have recognition, vision, a plan, and even diligence with hard work. But if your character isn't solid, everything will eventually collapse. Character is what holds up everything else. Talent opens doors, but only character keeps them open. Gifting gets you seen, but only integrity keeps you standing. Sometimes we don't realize how weak our foundation really is until we're standing under something heavy.

God knows this. He's more interested in your foundation than your platform. He's not just trying to give you influence, but He's making sure you don't get crushed by it. If you succeed before you're ready, the very blessing you prayed for can become the thing that breaks you. God cares more about your character than your comfort. He won't promote you just to watch you fall apart, because He loves you too much for that.

One verse in Proverbs warns us,

An inheritance gained hastily at the beginning will not be blessed at the end.

—Proverbs 20:21

The inheritance isn't bad, but it came too soon. When blessing comes before the foundation is tested, it won't last or hold. Either you'll lose it or, worse, it'll reveal something broken in you that was never healed in the secret place. God often withholds promotion not because He's punishing you but because He's protecting you. In the kingdom, character comes first. If the root system isn't deep enough, the fruit won't last.

You can plan, grind, network, build, hustle, fast, and believe all day. But if the internal structure of your life can't support what God's trying to build on it, the weight will crush you. This is why God is patient, allows testing, and brings correction. He's building something that's not supposed to collapse.

When character fails, it doesn't just damage your peace—it damages your prosperity.

## Bad Character Costs a Lot

When people think about the consequences of bad character, they usually consider personal terms: shame, guilt, regret. Those are real, but in the kingdom the stakes are even higher. Bad character doesn't just cost you emotionally. It costs you economically. It doesn't just touch your soul but touches your wealth, your future, your legacy. This isn't about feeling bad; it's about what you forfeit when you choose compromise over integrity.

Scripture warns us about this so clearly:

> Remove your way far from her...lest you give your honor to others, and your years to the cruel one; lest aliens be filled with your wealth, and your labors go to the house of a foreigner.

—Proverbs 5:8–10

This isn't just about sexual immorality but about any pattern of compromise that erodes your foundation. Scripture paints the picture: Your honor gets transferred to someone else; your labor gets consumed by someone who didn't earn it; and your wealth, years, and work all get swallowed by the consequences of unchecked sin. You lose what you spent years building. The cost of bad character isn't just spiritual; it's financial and generational.

I've seen it firsthand more times than I wish I had. I've pastored people through it and walked with leaders, entrepreneurs, creatives, and ministers who were anointed, gifted, and positioned for impact. Then it all unraveled. Not because they weren't called or lacked talent but because they didn't protect their character. They didn't guard their hearts or take small compromises seriously until those compromises snowballed into full collapse. By the time it all came to light, it wasn't just their peace that was gone; it was their income, reputation, marriage, team, and credibility. Years of work, swept away in a moment.

Sin always charges more than it advertises. You don't get to set the price. It costs you time, energy, trust, money, and years you can't get back. It's not enough to be talented or passionate. If you don't guard your character, you will eventually lose what your gifting helped you gain.

I've seen marriages fall apart because of adultery. What started as private compromise ended as public disaster: two mortgages, two sets of bills, two parents splitting time with their children. I've seen entrepreneurs manipulate clients, fudge numbers, cut corners, then collapse under lawsuits or IRS investigations. I've seen ministers who genuinely loved God but didn't set up guardrails in their private lives. When the secret came out, they didn't just lose their peace—they lost their voices, influence, and spiritual authority.

I need you to hear this: It always costs more than you think. Sin doesn't just rob you of sleep; it robs you of fruit, favor, and the very blessing you worked so hard to build. Once it starts costing you, you don't get to control how much it takes.

Character matters more than you think. It's about not just staying at peace with God but protecting what God has entrusted to you: your calling, resources, and ability to lead. If you don't guard your life, the enemy will drain your labor. That's not fear; that's Scripture. It's not a threat but an invitation to take your calling seriously enough to stay clean.

Guarding your doctrine is important, but if you don't also guard yourself, you'll lose both.

## Your Patterns Preach

Paul told Timothy, "Take heed to yourself and to the doctrine. Continue in them, for in doing this you will save both yourself and those who hear you" (1 Tim. 4:16). He didn't just say, "Watch your doctrine." He said, "Watch yourself." Watch how you live, walk, and handle power, pressure, and opportunity. What you do when no one's watching shapes what people see when they are. Your life is preaching louder than your sermon.

You don't just preach with your gifting—you preach with your discipline, calendar, and boundaries. Your life is always sending a message, whether you realize it or not. People are watching, listening, and following your patterns even more than your points. If your private life contradicts your public message, it will eventually crash down. Not because the message isn't good but because the messenger isn't guarded.

As Proverbs puts it,

> He who walks with integrity walks securely, but he who perverts his ways will become known.
>
> —Proverbs 10:9

You might fool people for a season or even fool yourself, but eventually, your character or lack of it will become known. It always does. God is not mocked. What's done in the dark always comes into the light. When that moment happens, your life will be either a testimony or a cautionary tale.

I've seen this up close: leaders who had all the right language, gifting, and momentum, but underneath the surface there were compromises. Those compromises eventually rose to the surface. When they did, the fallout wasn't just personal—it was public. Families were affected, churches were shaken, businesses were fractured. Not because the person didn't love God but because they didn't take seriously the responsibility of guarding their life.

Guarding your life is guarding your message. You can't separate the two. Your doctrine might be solid, but if your habits aren't, people will still stumble. If your theology is deep but your boundaries are weak, the fruit of your ministry will spoil. People don't just need to hear the truth; they need to *see* what it looks like lived out.

This isn't just about avoiding sin but about carrying yourself with integrity, walking in humility, and being accountable, honest, and clean behind closed doors. That's where legacy is built. If you're serious about building something that lasts, you can't just focus on what you're preaching. You have to take responsibility for how you're living.

When you choose to keep your hands clean and your heart right, God becomes your defender.

## God Will Fight for the Cleanhanded

I've lived through this test personally. I've had people wrong me financially: partners who defrauded me, contracts that were broken, individuals who promised blessing and delivered betrayal. Everything in me wanted to fight back, prove a point, make them pay, clear my name, and get justice. It would've felt justified and fair. But the Holy Spirit spoke to me clearly: "Keep your hands clean. Keep your heart clean. Trust Me to be your defender."

I had to make a choice. I chose the harder road: the one that didn't give me instant resolution, didn't let me take justice into my own hands, didn't give me the satisfaction of calling someone out publicly or trying to fix it through the flesh. I chose character over control, humility over retaliation, trust over vengeance.

I want to be honest: It wasn't easy. It's never easy. But every time I've taken that route, God has restored what was stolen. Not just eventually but *faithfully*. God has honored that posture and that decision to stay clean, to stay in integrity. Every time I did, I saw Him move on my behalf. He brought peace when I could've had drama, provision when I could've forced a fight, and justice without me having to lift a finger.

When you refuse to take matters into your own hands, God steps in. He says, "That one's Mine. I'll handle it." And He does, in ways you couldn't predict and on a timeline you couldn't control, but with fruit you never could've manufactured on your own. When you let go of offense and hold on to integrity, you give heaven something to work with.

You need to know this: God will defend the one who keeps their heart pure. He will fight for the one who refuses to fight dirty. The world tells you that you have to get even, clap back, and protect your name at all costs. But the kingdom works differently. In the kingdom, protection follows purity, vindication follows surrender, and justice comes to the one who stays quiet, stays low, and stays clean.

Character doesn't just preserve peace; *it preserves wealth.*

## Fast Money Fades—but Integrity Multiplies

Wealth gained the wrong way never lasts. You can chase fast money, manipulate the system, cut corners, and maybe even get ahead for a moment. But if it wasn't built on integrity, it won't stay. It might look like success on the surface, but underneath it's hollow. Eventually, it collapses.

According to Proverbs,

> Wealth gained by dishonesty will be diminished, but he who gathers by labor will increase.
>
> —Proverbs 13:11

If you try to build your business, ministry, or life by cutting corners, you will not be able to sustain it. It will dry up, unravel, and expose you. But if you gather by labor—if you build slow, steady, and honest—you *will* increase, not just financially. God will multiply your influence, trust, and capacity to steward more. It may not happen overnight or come with flashy headlines, but it will be *blessed*.

You have to decide what kind of increase you want. Do you want the kind that comes quickly and fades just as fast? Or do you want the kind that endures—fruit that remains? When you choose character, you're not just protecting your peace but building a foundation God can increase without limit. That's the blessing of integrity. It may slow you down in the short term, but it guarantees that what you're building won't fall apart when pressure hits.

I've seen this in so many stories: people who tried to win the fast way. They got the promotion but lost their credibility, scaled the business but lost their soul, got the money but couldn't keep it. Fast money doesn't make you fruitful; it makes you fragile. But when you walk in integrity, your roots go deep. When the storm hits, you're not shaken. You're still standing.

## Joseph and Daniel—the Blueprint for God's Promotion

If you want to build something that lasts, you need to study the people God raised up for more than just a moment. Two of the clearest examples in Scripture are Joseph and Daniel.

Throughout Scripture when God wants to entrust someone with influence, He always tests their character first. He doesn't just look at their skill; He looks at their heart. He examines how they handle pressure, betrayal, temptation, and obscurity. No two men model this more clearly than Joseph and Daniel.

Joseph was sold into slavery by his own brothers, lied about, falsely accused of sexual assault, thrown into prison, and forgotten for years. Yet *he never compromised*, never let bitterness poison him, never let injustice justify cutting corners. He didn't use his pain as an excuse to stop being excellent. He stayed faithful in the dark and served diligently in places where no one was clapping. When the day of elevation finally came, Pharaoh didn't just see Joseph's gift; he saw his *character*. Joseph didn't scheme his way into influence; he served his way there. God raised him up not just for Joseph's sake but for the sake of an entire nation.

The same thing happened with Daniel. He was taken captive to Babylon, stripped of his freedom, surrounded by compromise, and pressured to blend in. But Daniel refused to defile himself. He stayed clean in a dirty culture and kept praying when it became illegal to do so. Because he kept his character intact, God made him stand out. The Bible says Daniel and his friends were ten times wiser, ten times more excellent, ten times more favored than anyone else around them. (See Daniel 1:20.) Character multiplies what favor initiates.

These men weren't promoted because they were clever but because they were *clean*. They were trustworthy and faithful when no one was looking. They were tested before they were trusted. When God looked for someone to entrust with resources, authority, and influence, He didn't look for the flashiest—He looked for the faithful.

You may feel overlooked right now. You may feel like no one sees your diligence, values your integrity, or appreciates your quiet sacrifice. But heaven sees. God is watching. When He finds someone who refuses to compromise—who stays clean in the secret place—He lifts them up in the right time. Not for their glory but for His.

In the kingdom, character doesn't just protect what you build; it determines how high God can trust you to go.

If you compromise to climb, you will collapse under pressure. If you cut corners to win now, you will lose something more valuable later. But if you stay faithful—if you stay clean, humble, and aligned with the heart of God—He will build you into someone who can carry blessing without breaking. In the kingdom your *character* determines your capacity. It determines how much wealth you can be trusted with, how much influence you can steward, and how much fruit you can bear without rotting from the inside out.

The financial anointing, and every other kind of blessing, isn't built on charisma—it's built on character. I'm not just building for today; I'm building for legacy, for fruit that remains. If you're serious about stepping into everything God has for you, then you need to get serious about your character.

That's the law of character.

## REFLECTION QUESTIONS

1. What temptation could compromise your financial testimony if left unchecked?

2. How can integrity become your greatest asset in business and ministry?

3. What does it look like to prosper without losing your purity?

Pray this out loud:

*Lord, make me trustworthy with wealth. Purify my motives so prosperity never outruns my integrity. Let my success be anchored in holiness and humility so everything I build honors You. In Jesus' name, amen.*

To access additional resources, scan the QR code or visit thepowertoprosperbook.com/resources.

CHAPTER 16

# THE LAW OF APPEARANCE

THERE'S A STORY about a world-class violinist named Joshua Bell. One night, he played a $3.5 million violin for a packed theater. Tickets sold for hundreds of dollars, and the audience sat silently in awe.

Days later, he went to a subway station in Washington, DC, dressed in jeans and a baseball cap. He played the same violin and performed the same music. Over a thousand people walked by. Almost no one stopped. He made less than forty dollars.

The quality was identical, the value unchanged. The gift hadn't diminished. But the *appearance* changed everything. That's the law of appearance.

## Appearance Speaks Before You Do

Too many people in the church underestimate this law. They downplay its importance, excuse their sloppiness, and spiritualize their carelessness as if it makes them more holy. I've seen it repeatedly: people who love God, have genuine gifting, and even possess deep theology, but they walk into rooms with zero awareness of how they're presenting themselves.

They quote scriptures like "The LORD looks at the heart" (1 Sam. 16:7), and use it as an excuse to neglect how they look, carry themselves, or steward the spaces around them. What they forget is that 1 Samuel 16:7 also says that "man looks at the outward appearance." When you don't take that seriously, you'll misrepresent the very God you're trying to glorify.

Let me say it clearly: You can have recognition, vision, diligence, and character, but if your appearance communicates confusion, chaos, or carelessness, you'll close doors before your message gets heard. Your appearance speaks before you do. People make decisions about you in the first few seconds—before you preach, present, or post. If you look disorganized, distracted, or unintentional, they'll assume what you carry isn't worth listening to. It's not fair, but that's the world we live in. If you want to make an impact, you need to understand the system you're working in.

Here's the truth: Everything communicates something. Your body language, tone, face, lighting, grammar, captions, posture, voice inflection, YouTube thumbnail, podcast title, and welcome email. It's all preaching something. Even when you're not trying to communicate, you are. People hear that message long before they get to the one you intended to share.

This doesn't mean you need to be flashy or wear thousand-dollar outfits or luxury watches. I'm not advocating for some curated influencer aesthetic. What I'm saying is simple: How you show up matters. Whether you realize it or not, your appearance communicates something, and it's either working for you or working against you. It's either opening the door for your message or quietly convincing people they can walk away.

I'm saying this not to add pressure but to raise your level of stewardship. We live in a world that forms opinions quickly. When you don't take that seriously, you give people a reason to reject your message before they ever hear your heart. You might be carrying a word from heaven, but if your appearance says you're unprepared, people will tune out before they realize what they're missing.

That's the weight of appearance. It doesn't determine your worth, but it does affect your witness.

Appearance isn't about vanity. It's about good stewardship.

## Excellence Reflects the Kingdom

Excellence is not about impressing people. It's about representing the King of kings. When you carry God's presence, how you present yourself should reflect the nature of the God you serve. He is not sloppy, careless, or halfway. When you reflect Him with excellence, people take notice.

This is exactly what happened in 2 Chronicles 9. The queen of Sheba had heard rumors about Solomon's wisdom, wealth, and brilliance. But when she arrived, it wasn't just his words that left her breathless; it was how everything looked.

> When the queen of Sheba had seen the wisdom of Solomon, the house that he had built, the food on his table, the seating of his servants, the service of his waiters and their apparel...there was no more spirit in her.
>
> —2 Chronicles 9:3–4

She was undone. Not because Solomon preached or laid hands on her but because his excellence was everywhere. The food presentation, house design, staff appearance, and service quality all told a story. It wasn't just his spoken words but the atmosphere he created. The result? A woman from a distant land walked away in awe of God.

That's what appearance does when submitted to the kingdom—it preaches. It reveals what you believe. Whether you realize it or not, your environment speaks about your values. Your hospitality reflects your honor. Your level of excellence communicates your theology. Everything communicates something, and when excellence shows up, it tells people, "This message matters. This place matters. You matter."

Solomon didn't need to be flashy to reflect God. He just needed to be excellent. Excellence isn't perfection or spending money you don't have or keeping up with trends. It's about intentionality and care. It's stewarding life's details because the King of kings lives inside you, and people are watching how you represent Him.

When you don't take this seriously, your appearance won't just reflect sloppiness; it will send the wrong message entirely.

## Sloppiness Sends a Message

Most people don't intend to send the wrong message, but they do because they don't realize how much their sloppiness speaks. They assume their heart will shine through and people will overlook messy details to hear the Word. But that's not how influence works. You may have the best intentions, but if your delivery is chaotic, your audience won't trust what you're saying.

I've seen it too many times. The message was good, the theology solid, and the person clearly loved God. But the whole thing was hard to watch. The audio cut in and out. The camera angle was awkward. The captions were filled with typos. Instead of people leaning in, they checked out. Not because they didn't want truth but because the distraction was louder than the content.

Sloppiness doesn't just make things ugly; it makes them untrustworthy. When a room is disorganized, people don't feel at ease. When an email is full of errors, people second-guess the sender. When details are chaotic, people question credibility. They don't think, "This person must be deeply spiritual." They think, "This person doesn't have it together."

The tragedy is that sometimes these people carry exactly what their audience needs, but the message gets lost in the mess.

Remember, everything communicates something. Even what you don't intend to communicate speaks on your behalf. When you're careless with visuals, systems, language, lighting, or tone, you're not just missing a detail; you're misrepresenting a kingdom.

This isn't about being slick or corporate. This is about creating clarity and helping your message shine. It's about removing every barrier that would keep someone from receiving the truth God gave you to deliver. When your appearance aligns with your message's weight, it reinforces what you're saying. When it contradicts it, people disengage before they get to the point.

## Presentation Is a Form of Honor

How you present something reveals what you think about it and who it's for. Appearance isn't just about clarity; it's about honor. When you take time to prepare, be intentional, remove friction, and elevate the environment, you tell the recipient, "You matter. I value you."

I discovered this not as a branding strategy but as a spiritual principle. When I host people on my podcast, especially when they're flying in, I go out of my way to make the experience communicate value. I pay for flights, cover hotels, and take care of meals. Not to impress them or be flashy but because I want everything about the experience to say, "You're not just a guest. You're honored here."

I carry this same posture in preparing spaces, question writing, and following up. Presentation is about more than optics; it's showing people what you truly believe about them.

If you invite someone to your home and it's a mess, you're sending a message. If you host someone on your platform and the details are sloppy, you're sending a message. If you show up to a meeting late, distracted, and unprepared, you're still sending a message. If your business's website has terrible design, loads slowly, has irrelevant information, has broken links, and has a blog that hasn't been updated in three years, you're still sending a message. It's not just about how others see you but about how you see them. Do you see them as people, clients, customers, or congregants who are worth putting your best foot forward toward?

Honor is the decision to elevate someone through how you serve them. When Jesus washed His disciples' feet, it wasn't about optics; it was about posture. He wanted them to know, "This is how the kingdom works. This is what leadership looks like."

The same is true for how we present the gospel, prepare for ministry, build businesses, and show up in our assignments. Honor isn't just something you say; it's something you show.

## God Wants Everything You Present to Reflect Him

God doesn't separate the sacred from the practical. He doesn't just care about what you say in prayer; He cares about how you send an email. He doesn't just care about your heart in worship; He cares about your follow-through, hospitality, systems, graphics, and tone of voice. Everything you present either draws attention to Him or distracts people from Him. If you're called to represent heaven, that representation should show up in every detail.

This is what Jesus meant when He said, "Be wise as serpents and innocent as doves" (Matt. 10:16, ESV). We're sheep among wolves in a world that judges by appearance, even if we wish it didn't. We're not supposed to be naive about that; we're supposed to steward it wisely. This doesn't mean we compromise the message, but it does mean we present it with thoughtfulness, excellence, and kingdom weight. The world is watching. If the stewardship doesn't match the spiritual claim, people walk away.

Presentation matters not because we're obsessed with aesthetics but because we're obsessed with Jesus. We want people to see Him, not be distracted by us. Your systems are spiritual. Your workflows, documents, lighting, and booking process *all matter*—not just because they make you look professional but because they make you more prepared to honor the people God is sending your way.

God doesn't want you scrambling; He wants you structured. He wants what you present to reflect Him.

You may think, "It's just an Instagram post," but someone may scroll past and form an opinion about what you believe. You may think, "It's just a website," but that might be someone's first impression of the kingdom. You may think, "It's just a Zoom meeting," but that meeting may be when someone opens up to Jesus because of how safe, clear, and thoughtful you are with your presence. *Everything communicates something.* When you remember who you're representing, everything shifts.

## Your Appearance Can Preach the Gospel—or Undermine It

When you treat your skill and stewardship as an offering, your appearance doesn't just represent you; it opens doors for your message.

> Do you see a person skilled in his work? He will stand before kings; he will not stand before obscure people.
>
> —PROVERBS 22:29, NASB

There's something about skill and excellence that commands influence. When someone is diligent and intentional with what they present, doors open—not because they're chasing platform but because their stewardship attracts promotion. When you take your work seriously and show up skillfully, thoughtfully, and with intention, you won't stay in obscurity forever. People take notice. Opportunities find you. Your ability to represent the kingdom expands.

Your appearance can preach. It can say, "This message is worth hearing." It can communicate weight, reverence, clarity, and care. Or it can do the opposite, saying, "This was thrown together," or "This doesn't really matter," or "This person doesn't value their audience or assignment." When that's the case, people check out before you've had the chance to deliver what God gave you to say. They never hear the gospel, not because they rejected Jesus but because your presentation became a barrier.

You can't always control how people respond to truth, but you can control how you present it. In a world constantly bombarded with content, you have about three seconds to signal, "This is different. This is valuable. This is worth your attention." If what you're presenting doesn't match the weight of what you're carrying, it will quietly disqualify your message before it gets heard. This doesn't mean everything has to be perfect, but it should be intentional. God is excellent. If you're representing Him and claiming to carry a word from heaven, then your appearance should reflect that weight. Not in vanity or flash but in focus, care, and excellence.

People may never see your prayer life or hear how deeply you love God, but they will see how you show up. Your appearance will give them either a reason to listen or a reason to walk away.

Again, your appearance doesn't define your worth, but it influences your ability to be perceived as somebody worth investing in. You are a representative of heaven, an ambassador of the King. Everything you present tells the world something about the kingdom you belong to.

Don't neglect that. Don't downplay it. Don't hide behind spiritual excuses while your sloppiness undercuts your impact. In a world that forms conclusions before you speak, make sure your appearance says what you actually mean.

Carry yourself with clarity. Prepare with intention. Present with weight. Let everything about your life tell the world, "This message matters. This moment matters. This audience matters."

That's the law of appearance.

## REFLECTION QUESTIONS

1. How does your presentation—online and in person—reflect the excellence of the kingdom?

2. What practical improvements could make your brand, business, or ministry more credible?

3. How can your excellence preach the gospel before you ever say a word?

Pray this out loud:

*Father, You are excellent in all Your ways. Let that excellence shine through my life and work. Teach me to present myself, my message, and my mission with care that reflects Your glory. In Jesus' name, amen.*

To access additional resources, scan the QR code or visit thepowertoprosperbook.com/resources.

CHAPTER 17

# THE LAW OF SOWING AND REAPING

**T**HERE'S A STORY about a man named Percy Spencer, a poor farm boy from Maine who lost his parents young and left school after the fifth grade. He had no diploma, no formal training—just a hunger to learn. At night, he'd read electrical manuals by candlelight and tinker with scrap parts until something worked. Years later, while working as an engineer for Raytheon during World War II, he noticed something strange: A candy bar in his pocket had melted while he stood near an active radar magnetron. Most people would have brushed it off and moved on, but Percy didn't. He saw potential in what others ignored. That one small observation led to a series of experiments—and eventually, the invention of the microwave oven.

From an orphan with no education to the creator of a technology that transformed the modern world, Percy Spencer and his life prove that your seed doesn't have to be big to be powerful. It just has to be sown. When you work what's in your hand, God can multiply it beyond anything you imagined.

That's the law of sowing and reaping.

## Your Harvest Starts with Your Seed

If you don't plant anything, you shouldn't expect to harvest anything. If you sow a little, you'll reap a little. If you sow generously, you'll reap generously. And if you sow in faith, you'll reap in joy.

But everything—everything—starts with a seed.

The first time we see this law introduced is in Genesis 8:22. After the flood, God made a covenant with Noah, and part of that covenant was this promise:

> While the earth remains, seedtime and harvest, cold and heat, winter and summer, and day and night shall not cease.
>
> —GENESIS 8:22

It's built into the created order. Seedtime and harvest are as certain as sunrise and sunset. That means it's not just a metaphor; it's a law. As long as the earth exists, this principle is active.

When you learn to work with it (not fight it, resist it, or ignore it), you tap into a force that God Himself established as part of His divine system of increase.

A lot of Christians are praying for a harvest, but they've never actually sown seed. They're begging God to provide while holding tightly to what He's already placed in their hands.

The question is, What are you expecting God to multiply if you've never planted anything?

I'm not saying this to be harsh; I'm saying it to set people free because this law, once you understand it, will unlock you.

## How You Sow Determines How You Reap

If you want to walk in financial anointing, you have to stop praying like a beggar and start sowing like a builder. Seed is not just about generosity; it's about stewardship. It's about saying, "God, I trust You more than I trust the forecast." It's believing that what leaves your hand never leaves your life; it goes into your future and meets you there with a multiplied return.

The apostle Paul made this so clear in 2 Corinthians 9:6:

> But this I say: He who sows sparingly will also reap sparingly, and he who sows bountifully will also reap bountifully.

It's not an emotional appeal or a prosperity gimmick. It's a kingdom law. The way you sow determines the way you reap.

I'm not just talking about money. This applies to your time, relationships, energy, and prayers. Everything. But in the context of this chapter, we are specifically talking about sowing financially because this is one of the clearest areas where the church has failed to activate what God has provided.

Let me be clear: You cannot buy a miracle. You cannot buy healing. You cannot buy your way into favor. That's not what sowing is about.

But what you *can* do is participate in the system God designed, and when you do, you position yourself for overflow. Not because you earned it but because you honored His Word.

Sowing is not manipulation; it's participation.

You're not giving to twist God's arm. You're giving in agreement with how He already promised to move. That's why Jesus said,

> Give, and it will be given to you: good measure, pressed down, shaken together, and running over.
>
> —Luke 6:38

Not just enough for you—more than enough for others. That's what happens when you sow. God doesn't just meet your needs; He overflows them. He gives you seed for sowing, bread for eating, and surplus for impact.

## Sow in Tears—Reap in Joy

You might think, "Well, Kap, I'm in a dry season. Now's not a good time to give." But can I remind you of Isaac's example? He sowed in the midst of famine, not in abundance. And that same year, he reaped a supernatural increase.

He didn't wait for the market to turn. He didn't wait for the economy to bounce back.

He sowed in famine. He sowed in faith. And God responded.

The same is true for you. If you're waiting for things to be easy before you sow, you'll never sow. Sowing doesn't happen when it's easy; it happens when you trust God more than you trust your budget.

Even if it costs you something emotionally, even if it feels like a stretch, there's still a promise attached:

> Those who sow in tears shall reap in joy.
>
> —Psalm 126:5

I've lived this. I've sown in tears. I've written checks that scared me. I've given offerings that made no sense to my flesh. I've sold large assets that represented security for my own children in order to invest those resources into the vision God gave me for a new business. And God has brought it back: multiplied, blessed, and right on time. Every. Single. Time.

I've had people in my ministry experience the same thing. They stepped out in faith and sowed financially when it didn't make sense. Within weeks, they were promoted, blessed, and provided for in ways they never saw coming.

Not because I promised it. But because *God* did.

Here's the key: You don't sow when you feel it; you sow when you *believe* it. You sow in faith. You sow in alignment with God's principles. When you do, harvest is guaranteed. Not because of you but because of Him.

That's the law of sowing and reaping. And it's still in effect. While the earth remains, this law will not cease. So if you're tired of living from miracle to miracle, if you're tired of financially just surviving, if you're ready to build something that grows and overflows, then it's time to stop eating all your seed. It's time to plant. And when you do, you won't just reap in return. You'll reap in joy.

## REFLECTION QUESTIONS

1. What seed—financial, creative, or relational—has God asked you to plant?

2. In what ways have you been consuming what should have been sown?

3. What field is God calling you to invest in for long-term multiplication?

Pray this out loud:

*Lord, I release what's in my hand so You can release what's in Yours. Teach me to sow strategically, expectantly, and joyfully. I believe every seed I plant in faith will multiply for kingdom impact and generational blessing. In Jesus' name, amen.*

To access additional resources, scan the QR code or visit thepowertoprosperbook.com/resources.

CHAPTER 18

# THE LAW OF THE TITHE

L ET ME TELL you the story of a man named David Green, the founder of Hobby Lobby. In 1970 he started making picture frames in his garage with a six-hundred-dollar loan and a simple conviction: Every dollar that came in would honor God first. From the very beginning, he tithed—not just personally but through his business. As Hobby Lobby grew from a small family start-up into a multibillion-dollar company with more than one thousand stores and tens of thousands of employees, that principle never changed. Green committed a portion of every profit to fund churches, missionaries, and Bible distribution around the world. Decades later, he even gave away 100 percent of the company's ownership to ensure its profits would always serve God's purposes. His story proves that when you put God first in your finances, He doesn't just bless your income; He blesses your impact.

That's the law of the tithe.

## Tithing Is Worship

For many believers today, this is the law they've either overlooked, minimized, or reasoned away. They say things like, "That's Old Testament," or "I can't afford to tithe yet," or "I give God my time and talents instead." But the truth is, tithing isn't about what you feel ready for. It's not about legalism or obligation. It's about covenant. It's about putting God first and trusting Him to take care of the rest.

The tithe isn't a tip or a charitable donation. It's not something you do when you feel emotionally moved. The tithe is the first 10 percent of your increase brought to the Lord as an act of honor. God established it not as a request for when it's convenient but as a system for blessing and provision.

> Honor the LORD with your possessions, and with the firstfruits of all your increase; so your barns will be filled with plenty, and your vats will overflow with new wine.
>
> —PROVERBS 3:9–10

There's a direct connection here. You honor God with the first, and He honors you with the overflow. You don't tithe after everything else is paid or once you're "ahead." You tithe first because tithing isn't about what you have but about who you trust.

The tithe didn't start with the Law of Moses, but much earlier, with Abraham. Hundreds of years before the Mosaic Law was written, Abraham voluntarily tithed to Melchizedek, a priest of God Most High. He did it without being commanded, without a written statute, without religious pressure. Abraham recognized that every victory, blessing, and breakthrough he experienced came from God.

When Abraham tithed, he didn't tithe on the net income or wait to pay his men first. He didn't deduct travel expenses or transaction fees. He tithed on the gross, honoring God first. Before anyone else received anything from the spoils, Abraham took the first tenth and laid it before the priest as an act of worship.

> And he gave him a tithe of all.
>
> —GENESIS 14:20

This matters because it shows that tithing is not a law issue but a heart issue, a faith issue, a covenant issue. Abraham wasn't trying to earn something from God; he was honoring the God who had already blessed him. If Abraham, the father of our faith, tithed before the Law was ever instituted, how much more should we, who walk by faith today, honor this principle?

Some Christians argue, "But that was Old Testament. Jesus never commanded us to tithe." That's simply not true. Jesus explicitly affirmed the tithe in Matthew 23:23, when He rebuked the Pharisees for their legalism. They focused on tiny details like tithing even their spices while neglecting justice, mercy, and faith. But Jesus didn't cancel tithing; He clarified the priority:

> These you ought to have done, without leaving the others undone.
>
> —MATTHEW 23:23

In other words, yes, you should tithe. Yes, you should give God the first and the best. But you should also walk in love, justice, and mercy. Jesus didn't throw out the tithe; He repositioned it. He reminded us that tithing should flow from a heart that loves God, trusts God, and walks in obedience, not from religious obligation but from relational covenant.

## Tithing Is Warfare

When you tithe, you're making a statement to heaven and hell: "God, You're still first. I recognize You as my source. I trust You above the economy, above my paycheck, above my budget. You are my provider, and this tithe proves it."

That's why tithing is spiritual warfare. It breaks the spirit of mammon off your life. It breaks fear, greed, and self-reliance. Every time you bring your first and best to God, you come out of agreement with the world's system and reaffirm your agreement with the kingdom.

This covenant comes with a promise:

> "Bring all the tithes into the storehouse...and try Me now in this," says the LORD of hosts, "If I will not open for you the windows of heaven and pour out for you such blessing that there will not be room enough to receive it."
>
> —MALACHI 3:10

It's the only place in Scripture where God says, "Test Me." Everywhere else we are commanded not to test God. But when it comes to the tithe, He flips the script: "Try Me. Test Me. See if I'm not faithful." The promise isn't just survival but surplus. Not just enough to scrape by but overflow that you can't contain.

But the order matters. The tithe comes first. The blessing follows.

You don't wait until the windows of heaven open to start trusting God. You trust Him now. You honor Him now. You bring Him the first and the best, and you watch what He does with it.

When your pastors are properly teaching tithing, it's not from a motivation of manipulation or warped "prosperity gospel" theology. It's about our covenant with God, His lordship over what He's entrusted to us, and our trust in His ability to provide for us, again. Every time you tithe, you're building a foundation of honor that heaven can bless.

And as you can see, I haven't said tithing is the only key to prosperity. But I am saying this: If you're asking God for financial anointing while refusing to obey Him in the tithe, you are cutting yourself off from a blessing that He wants to give you.

Because God doesn't bless what you withhold. He blesses what you surrender.

That's the law of the tithe.

## REFLECTION QUESTIONS

1. How does tithing prove that God—not your paycheck—is your source?

2. What would change in your finances if you treated the tithe as worship, not obligation?

3. How can you teach this principle to the next generation so wealth remains holy?

Pray this out loud:

*God, I return the first and best to You. My tithe is my covenant declaration that You alone give me power to get wealth. Open the windows of heaven over my life, and let my obedience testify of Your faithfulness. In Jesus' name, amen.*

To access additional resources, scan the QR code or visit thepowertoprosperbook.com/resources.

## CHAPTER 19

# THE LAW OF GENEROSITY

**T**HERE'S A STORY about a man named Alan Barnhart, a businessman from Tennessee who built one of the largest crane and heavy-transport companies in America. When he and his brother took over their small family business in the 1980s, they made a covenant with God to cap their incomes and give the rest away. Over the next four decades, that little company grew into a nationwide enterprise with more than fifty branches, 1,500 employees, and hundreds of millions in annual revenue—all dedicated to kingdom impact. The Barnharts eventually gave 100 percent of the company's stock to charity, funneling its profits into missions and humanitarian work around the world. Regarding the company, Alan has often said something along the lines of, "We didn't want to build a kingdom for ourselves—we wanted to build the kingdom of God." His story proves that when you release what's in your hand, God multiplies what's in your reach.

That's the law of generosity.

You'll never walk in full prosperity until you understand this law: Generosity is not a suggestion; it's a system. It's the foundation of kingdom economics, the gateway to multiplication, and the evidence that you've been delivered from the spirit of mammon.

> Give, and it will be given to you: good measure, pressed down, shaken together, and running over.
>
> —LUKE 6:38

Jesus was not trying to be poetic. He's making a *financial promise*. Because in the kingdom the flow doesn't start until you sow.

## The Principle Goes Back to Genesis

Long before the law, before Israel, before the church, there was a seed. As we've covered, God said:

131

> As long as the earth endures, seedtime and harvest...will never cease.
>
> —GENESIS 8:22, NIV

This is the rhythm God set in motion from the beginning. Everything He blesses, He expects to be multiplied. Multiplication always begins with surrender.

When you put seed in the ground, it looks like loss. In fact, Jesus said that the seed must die in the soil, but before what?

Before it multiplies.

You see, in the kingdom every surrender sets up a supernatural return.

## The Proverbs 31 Woman Was a Giver

The Proverbs 31 woman exemplifies this principle:

> She extends her hand to the poor, yes, she reaches out her hands to the needy.
>
> —PROVERBS 31:20

She didn't just create wealth; *she re-created it in others*. She didn't just build for herself, but she became a blessing to others. That's what separates kingdom prosperity from carnal success. In the world wealth is about status. In the kingdom wealth is about supply.

## My Breakthrough with Giving

There was a time when giving felt like a burden to me. I wanted to be generous, but I also felt like I was barely keeping up. I remember going to Christian concerts where they would always stop the set to tell us about how we could sponsor a child in destitution somewhere around the world. And while the volunteers in orange vests walked the aisles to give donation envelopes to those interested in helping, my stomach would turn in knots. Man, I just wanted to honor my Father and be a blessing to these kids...but I felt like I was hardly a blessing to my own. I ended up giving, but man, it felt like a sacrifice. I'm embarrassed to say it felt more like an obligation than an overflow of compassion. I knew that wasn't God's desire for my giving.

I knew God was calling me to trust Him, truly.

So I started sowing more before it made sense, tithing before it was convenient, giving to ministries that fed me even when I felt like I needed help myself. Something happened as I stepped into this rhythm.

I stopped feeling like a victim and started walking like a vessel. Provision began showing up in ways I didn't expect—not just financially but relationally, spiritually, and strategically. God was training me in a powerful truth: "If I can get it through you, I can get it to you."

## Giving Is Not Losing

This revelation of God's promises changes everything, but so few really believe it. They've been conditioned to think that giving is subtraction, that it sets them back. But in the kingdom, giving is multiplication in disguise.

> One gives freely, yet grows all the richer; another withholds what he should give, and only suffers want.
>
> —PROVERBS 11:24, ESV

God's math makes no sense to the world, but it makes miracles for those who trust Him. You don't give to *get rich*. You give because you *are rich*, in faith, in identity, in revelation, and—because your Father is El Shaddai, the "All Sufficient One"—in resources too. As you give, you grow.

## You're Not a Lake—You're a River

God isn't looking for people to store the blessing; He's looking for people to *release it*. Lakes collect, but rivers flow. The more generous you are, the more God can entrust to you because He knows it won't stop with you.

> A generous person will be prosperous, and one who gives others… water will himself be given plenty.
>
> —PROVERBS 11:25, NASB

Generosity doesn't just meet the needs of others; it meets your own.

## Final Charge

If you want to prosper, get serious about sowing. Not out of pressure or manipulation but out of partnership with God's system.

Sow into ministries that feed your spirit. Sow into people who carry what you want to walk in. Sow where you're growing, and sow with faith and expectation.

The world says, "Hold on to what you have." Heaven says, "Release it and watch it return." Because the moment you release your seed, you authorize the flow.

That's the law of generosity.

## REFLECTION QUESTIONS

1. Who could encounter God's goodness through your next act of giving?

2. How might generosity expand your capacity for increase?

3. In what ways can you shift from being a bucket that collects to a river that flows?

Pray this out loud:

*Father, make me a vessel You can trust. Let generosity flow through me like a river that never runs dry. Break every trace of fear and selfishness, and multiply what I release for Your kingdom and Your glory. In Jesus' name, amen.*

To access additional resources, scan the QR code or visit thepowertoprosperbook.com/resources.

## CHAPTER 20

# THE LAW OF EXPANSION

LET ME TELL you about a woman named Madam C. J. Walker, America's first self-made female millionaire. She started with nothing—born to formerly enslaved parents, orphaned at seven, and working as a washerwoman for about a dollar a day. But she had a vision bigger than herself. When she discovered a formula that could help Black women restore and care for their hair, she didn't just see a product; she saw an opportunity to lift an entire community. She built a factory, a beauty school, and a national sales force that grew to include more than twenty thousand trained agents across the United States, Central America, and the Caribbean. Her company, Madam C. J. Walker Manufacturing Company, became a multimillion-dollar enterprise at a time when women—especially Black women—had almost no access to economic power. But her expansion was driven not by greed but by generosity. She saw growth as a way to multiply dignity, not just dollars.

That's the law of expansion.

## Don't Just Maintain—Multiply

God is in the business of increase. All throughout Scripture you see multiplication, enlargement, and fruitfulness. Every time He pours out a blessing or releases supernatural provision, He's looking for one thing: capacity. Did you prepare for this? Did you build enough room? Did you stretch? Did you make space for what He wanted to send?

God rewards the one who multiplies, and He honors those who *build*. He isn't looking to invest more into people who are just trying to maintain what they've already got. He's looking for sons and daughters who think like builders, who think like stewards, who understand that if God gave it to you, He expects you to do something with it. Not just protect it—*multiply it*.

Jesus taught this with a parable. A master goes on a trip and entrusts his wealth to three different servants. One gets five talents. One gets two.

One gets one. The first two servants get to work immediately. They don't sit on what they've been given or play it safe. They begin looking for ways to grow what they've been entrusted with. When the master returns, he praises them and gives them *more*. Why? Because they were faithful with a little, and they were *focused* on expansion.

But the third servant buried what he received. Fear held him back. Instead of multiplying it, he hid it. When the master returned, he wasn't just disappointed; he was *furious*:

> You ought to have deposited my money with the bankers, and at my coming I would have received back my own with interest....Cast the unprofitable servant into the outer darkness.
>
> —Matthew 25:27, 30

That's a strong word, but it shows us something important: Playing it safe doesn't please God. More than that, according to Jesus, it's damnable. Maintaining doesn't fulfill God's mandate to multiply. If you're burying what God has given you out of fear, passivity, or excuses, you're disqualifying yourself from increase.

## Isaiah 54: Prepare for Increase

Now contrast that with Isaiah 54, one of the most prophetic passages in all Scripture when it comes to expansion. It's God calling His people to *prepare* for blessing.

> Enlarge the place of your tent, and let them stretch out the curtains of your dwellings; do not spare; lengthen your cords, and strengthen your stakes. For you shall expand to the right and to the left, and your descendants will inherit the nations.
>
> —Isaiah 54:2–3

The word here is *enlarge*. Stretch out. Build an addition. Spare *no* expense. God doesn't say, "I'm going to bless you, then you'll figure it out." He says, "Get ready *now*. Make space *now*. Build capacity *now*." When the blessing comes, you don't want it to break you. You want to be ready to sustain it.

This became deeply personal for me in 2025. I remember it so clearly, when the Lord brought me back to Isaiah 54 and said, "Kap, I want to bless your ministry and your business, but your infrastructure can't handle what I want to give you. You're asking Me to send more people, but you're not serving well enough the ones I've already sent. How can I entrust you with more if you're barely managing the current load?"

That hit me hard. I was praying for expansion without preparing for it. I was praying for souls without building systems to disciple them. I was believing for financial increase without restructuring the back end of my ministry to handle it with integrity and scale. So God called me to build.

I invested everything. I poured my own money into a new studio so I could produce long-form interviews, develop teaching content, and reach more people with the gospel. I bought new equipment, brought on new team members, upgraded software, and streamlined operations. I also restructured my entire business from an agency to a coaching business that trains other business leaders to use their platforms to win souls like I did. This wasn't just about quality; it was about capacity. It was about preparing the nets before the fish showed up.

Here's what's amazing: As we were building and spending, God was *providing*. It didn't make sense on paper, but I could feel it in my spirit. This is how kingdom expansion works. When you move in faith, God fills what you build and blesses what you stretch. Jesus told Peter,

> "Launch out into the deep and let down your nets for a catch."…They caught a great number of fish, and their net was breaking.…They signaled to their partners.…And they came and filled both the boats.
> —LUKE 5:4–7

Peter didn't just catch fish for himself. His obedience created *overflow* so abundant that he had to call in others. The harvest was bigger than his boat, bigger than his net. His expansion became someone else's blessing. That's what kingdom growth is supposed to do. It doesn't stop with you; it makes room for others.

## Expand Beyond Yourself

You need a vision that's bigger than you. If your dream ends with your own house, your own paycheck, your own peace of mind, it's too small. God is looking for builders who think *beyond themselves*, people who say, "Lord, give me more—not so I can live comfortably but so I can bring more people in." That's what Peter's partners experienced. That's what kingdom expansion creates.

I've experienced this personally. When I was on a mission trip in Colombia, I connected with a friend who pastors a church there. He had been struggling financially and asked if I had any ideas. As I considered it, the Lord gave me an idea—not just to give him advice but to expand my ministry in a way that could bless his family. I realized his wife had incredible administrative gifts, and I hired her to work remotely with my ministry. That decision didn't just bless them; it blessed me. It created capacity and allowed me to focus on the areas I'm uniquely called to, while empowering others to step into their assignments.

Since then I've expanded the team even more: content creators, content managers, a chief of staff, a coaching program for kingdom entrepreneurs and ministers. We're building bigger nets so that when the harvest comes, we can catch it without breaking.

The early church faced the same challenge. In Acts 6 the disciples were multiplying. Needs were increasing. The momentum was real, but the system wasn't ready. The apostles had a decision to make: Would they try to carry everything themselves, or would they release others to carry the weight?

> Seek out from among you seven men of good reputation, full of the
> Holy Spirit...whom we may appoint over this business; but we will
> give ourselves continually to prayer and to the ministry of the word.
> —Acts 6:3–4

They chose multiplication. They delegated and elevated because the vision had outgrown their personal capacity. Instead of controlling it, they expanded the team, raised up leaders, and shared the load. Because of that, the church didn't stall; it soared.

The same principle shows up in the life of Moses. He was leading Israel through the wilderness, trying to answer every question, solve every problem, mediate every dispute. But it was too much. Jethro, his father-in-law, told him straight:

The thing that you do is not good....Select from all the people able men....And let them judge the people at all times....It will be easier for you, for they will bear the burden with you.

—Exodus 18:17, 21–22

In other words, delegate and elevate. Build systems. Multiply leaders. Stretch out the tent. Expansion isn't selfish when it's rooted in kingdom purpose; it's sacred stewardship.

In the kingdom, expansion isn't about empire building. It's about capacity for souls. It's about creating jobs for people who would otherwise be stuck in secular systems. It's about creating opportunities for others to walk into their destinies.

Expansion demands faith, risk, and sacrifice. But if you're willing to build for others and not just yourself, God will bless it.

That's the law of expansion.

## REFLECTION QUESTIONS

1. What new territory is God asking you to occupy for His glory?

2. How can growth in your business or ministry create jobs and disciples?

3. What fear of risk do you need to trade for faith in God's limitless supply?

Pray this out loud:

*Lord, stretch my capacity and enlarge my vision. Give me courage to build beyond comfort. Let my expansion bring others into prosperity and reveal Your covenant to the world. In Jesus' name, amen.*

To access additional resources, scan the QR code or visit thepowertoprosperbook.com/resources.

## CHAPTER 21

# THE LAW OF FAMILY

THERE'S A STORY about a man named Eric Yuan, the founder of Zoom. Years before his company became a household name, Yuan was offered a series of high-paying promotions that required constant travel. But he quietly turned them down—because he didn't want to miss dinner with his kids. He built his business around family, not in spite of it. When work and home came into conflict, his rule was simple: Family wins. Years later, that same conviction became the foundation of a company that connected the world. Zoom grew from a start-up into a multibillion-dollar enterprise, serving hundreds of millions of users daily across more than 180 countries. The very principle that made Yuan protect his own home became the reason his company helped millions of others stay connected to theirs.

That's the law of family.

This is where a lot of people get ambition wrong, even godly ambition. They think that sacrificing their family is somehow a holy thing, that being "sold out" for God means leaving their spouse, their kids, and their household behind to pursue ministry at any cost. What I've seen over and over again is that this kind of thinking doesn't produce righteousness. It produces rebellion or religion. God doesn't want either.

You may have grown up watching this firsthand. Your parents put ministry above family. Maybe they were pastors or missionaries. Maybe they just volunteered for everything at church. Every time you needed them, they weren't there because they were too busy "serving the Lord." What they were actually doing, without realizing it, was putting you on the altar of sacrifice. Now you carry the wounds of that, or worse, you've started repeating the cycle in your own family.

Let me be as clear as I can: That's not God. That's not the heart of the Father, and that's not how kingdom prosperity works. God doesn't call you to win the world and lose your household. He calls you to shepherd your household first. He calls you to provide and prioritize. If you neglect that, you disqualify yourself from the rest of it.

The Bible doesn't pull punches about this either. Look at what Paul wrote:

> But if anyone does not provide for his own, and especially for those of his household, he has denied the faith and is worse than an unbeliever.
>
> —1 Timothy 5:8

That's strong language. "Denied the faith." "Worse than an unbeliever." Why? Because when God saves you, He doesn't just give you a pulpit. He gives you responsibility. He expects you to steward your family like a gift, not abandon them in the name of calling.

I've heard people say, "Well, the church will take care of my kids." No. That's not how it works. God didn't give the youth pastor authority over your family; He gave it to you. The same spirit that says, "The church should disciple my kids," was alive in Paul's day, when people were burdening the church to care for their family members because they didn't want to. Paul sharply rebuked them for it.

This law matters because if you get this wrong, nothing else you build will last. You'll have a platform but no peace at home. Applause, but no intimacy. I'm telling you, the world doesn't need another gifted preacher with a broken family. The world needs examples of men and women who love God and love their families, who know how to balance their calling to the crowds with their primary ministry at home.

Now, this isn't to condemn anybody. If you're working your tail off at one or multiple jobs to provide for your family and you're not able to be home because you're working so hard, God has grace for you. There's mercy for you. But I also want to encourage you: God's will for you is not that you would stay stuck there. God doesn't want you chasing the bag so helplessly that you can't take care of your family. Sacrifice like that can work for a season, but not as a continuous lifestyle. Otherwise, your calling will soon feel like a life sentence.

And I don't believe that's God's desire for you. I believe what the Bible says:

> The blessing of the LORD makes one rich, and He adds no sorrow with it.
>
> —Proverbs 10:22

That's God's heart. God doesn't bless you at the expense of your peace. He doesn't want you building wealth while your kids grow up not knowing who you are. He doesn't want you funding ministry while your spouse is drowning emotionally at home. The Word is clear: The blessing of God comes without sorrow attached.

But when you chase money for money's sake, when you do things your own way and call it "providing," the Bible shows us what happens:

> For the love of money is a root of all kinds of evil, for which some have strayed from the faith in their greediness, and pierced themselves through with many sorrows.
>
> —1 Timothy 6:10

That's what the devil does. He always wants a trade. He'll say, "Yeah, I'll bless your business. But I want your family. Yeah, I'll give you more clients. But I want your sleep. Yeah, I'll increase your income. But I want your marriage." That's how he works.

But God doesn't operate like that. God doesn't do trades. God blesses richly with no asterisks or fine print attached.

## The Blessing of Righteous Prioritization

When you pursue God and obey Him, walking in lockstep with Him, how many scriptures do you need that clearly lay out how your obedience will be blessed? If you seek first the kingdom of God and His righteousness, all these things will be added to you. Your cup will run over. You'll have no needs. You're called to meet needs. It's all over Scripture. It's a promise.

When you obey God and receive His blessing without making trades with the devil, you understand that God doesn't want any trades. He wants covenant. What is *covenant? Covenant* means a promise that's unbreakable because of your relationship.

> And you shall remember the LORD your God, for it is He who gives you power to get wealth, that He may establish His covenant which He swore to your fathers, as it is this day.
>
> —Deuteronomy 8:18

God wants you to prosper not apart from your family but with your family. He wants your family blessed, whole, and in the picture. When

God blesses you, He doesn't bless one branch of your life while letting all the others wither. He wants *all of it* blessed.

Take care of your family. Provide for your family. Focus on blessing your family and being a blessing to them. *Bless your spouse.* One of the best pieces of pastoral advice I've ever received was this: "When it comes to planning the budget, be very generous to your wife. Whatever she needs."

If she needs to feel good about herself and says, "I've got to go get my nails done. I've got to get my hair done," take care of those things. Take care of your wife because *she's your own body.* Bless her, and it will come back to you.

Blessing your family and taking care of them will be rewarded by God. God wants you to be a person who's taking care of your family. Make sure your kids get time with you. You might not have the capacity or financial means for some crazy vacation, but take time away. Invest in your family. Press pause.

If you continue saying, "I can't afford that," you'll never do it, and it'll actually cost you more in the long run. "I can't afford to take my wife on a date. I can't afford to do fun things with my kids." You know what's free? The park. Take your family on a picnic. Do something. *Invest in your family.* This is what God wants you to do.

## No Sorrow

Let's look at Proverbs 10:22 one more time:

> The blessing of the LORD makes one rich, and He adds no sorrow with it.

When you pursue God, obeying Him and walking in alignment with Him, there's no sorrow attached to the blessing. That's how God works. He doesn't want to bless your bank account at the cost of your soul. He doesn't want to bless your platform at the cost of your peace. God blesses you, but not at the expense of your marriage, your kids, your health, or your sanity. That's not how He operates.

You see the contrast? The blessing of the Lord makes you rich and adds no sorrow. But chasing after money—loving money—will pierce you. It will wound you and rob you. The devil doesn't care how much money you make as long as you lose what matters in the process.

But our covenant-making God doesn't need to negotiate. He doesn't come to the table saying, "If you give Me your family, I'll give you increase." No—He blesses your whole house. He blesses all of you. He gives you wealth and peace and legacy. He expects you to steward it all, not trade one for the other.

That's why this law matters. When you understand that God wants your whole life blessed, not just your income, you stop making compromises. You stop trading time with your kids for a few more hours at the office. You stop trading the health of your marriage for the illusion of financial progress. You stop thinking that prosperity has to come at a price and start believing that prosperity is part of God's covenant.

God wants every branch in your life to prosper. He wants your family to do well. If you honor Him and honor your family, it will go well for you.

First Timothy chapter 3 says that anybody who wants to be a leader in the church—a bishop, deacon, or pastor—desires a good thing. That's godly ambition. But anyone in church leadership must go through qualifications first. One qualification is that they must manage their household well. (See 1 Timothy 3:1–13.) If you can't manage your household well, how are you going to manage the house of God? How are you going to manage a business with employees?

God doesn't want you to put your family on the altar of doing work for Him. He wants your family to thrive. He wants your family not to resent ministry but to look at it as a massive privilege they get to be part of, knowing that God is a rewarder. Because He is.

# REFLECTION QUESTIONS

1. How can your pursuit of prosperity better serve your spouse and children?

2. Where do you need to restore order between work, wealth, and home?

3. How will your financial obedience build generational blessing instead of burnout?

Pray this out loud:

*Father, bless my household. Teach me to lead with love, provide with wisdom, and prosper without neglect. Let our family become a living example of covenant wealth that glorifies You. In Jesus' name, amen.*

To access additional resources, scan the QR code or visit thepowertoprosperbook.com/resources.

# CHAPTER 22

# THE LAW OF CONTENTMENT

THERE'S A STORY about Corrie ten Boom that always moves me. She was imprisoned in a Nazi concentration camp for hiding Jews during the Holocaust. In one of the most brutal, inhumane places on earth, she and her sister Betsie were crammed into a filthy barrack crawling with lice. At one point, Corrie cried out in frustration about the infestation, only to hear her sister thank God for the lice. Corrie couldn't believe it. "Why would you thank God for lice?" she asked.

Later they discovered that the lice had actually kept the guards away from their barrack, allowing them to hold Bible studies without interruption. That moment was a revelation: Contentment isn't about the conditions around you; it's about the gratitude within you.

What I've discovered is that gratitude multiplies things. Gratitude is a magnet for increase. But discontentment—this chronic craving for what's next—actually keeps you from receiving what God wants to give. You cannot walk in supernatural provision if you're blinded by entitlement. God is not in a hurry to give more to someone who isn't even thankful for what they already have. Discontentment is a losing, victim mentality that keeps you from prospering. But contentment and gratitude, that mindset is one of the most irrefutable ingredients for winning.

You see the difference? God's not looking for whiners; He's looking for *winners*. And contentment is an emphatic proclamation that you've already won and you're ready for more.

That's the law of contentment.

## Gratitude Multiplies; Greed Subtracts

Here's what I've discovered in life: Gratitude multiplies things. Gratitude and contentment are magnets for multiplication. I don't think God is very motivated to increase people who are not grateful. He is very motivated to increase people who are grateful.

146

Think about it the same way as a parent. If my kids just look at me as a lottery ticket or an ATM or a genie, and if I'm just giving them things and they're not going to say thank you, I'm not very motivated to keep increasing their lives. I'm not motivated to keep blessing them with stuff or experiences or whatever else.

But when they're grateful, when they show me, "Dad, I'm so grateful you got me that Lego set. It's so fun. Can I show you it? Can we do this together?" I'm like, "Heck yeah, that's a kid I want to bless," because they're grateful. They're content. They don't need much, but it makes me want to pour out the blessing on them. I don't want to withhold blessing from them. And I'm an imperfect dad.

How much more does our perfect, heavenly Father want to bless those that are grateful?

Let's go to John 6:11:

> And Jesus took the loaves, and when He had given thanks He distributed them to the disciples, and the disciples to those sitting down; and likewise of the fish, as much as they wanted.

Do you see what happened? This is the story when thousands of people were following them. They all were hungry, and the disciples didn't know how to feed these people. So the disciples were like, "Yo, Jesus, what do we do? We don't have enough money to feed these people. Should we tell them to go home and get their own lunches?"

Jesus responded, "No. Whatever you've got, bring it here." So this little boy came up with five loaves of bread and two fish. Look at the first thing Jesus did before He started trying to make something of it: He gave thanks.

Jesus took the loaves, and when He had given thanks, He distributed them. *Gratitude multiplies.*

Before you begin asking God for a breakthrough, before you begin asking God for vision and wisdom for your business (there's nothing wrong with asking for those things), stop and give thanks.

"God, thank You for meeting my needs today. Thank You, God, that I have great clothes on. Thank You, God, that I have a great office to work in. Thank You, God, that my Wi-Fi is working. Thank You, Lord, that my family is healthy. Thank You, Lord, that You speak to me. Thank You, Lord. I'm just so grateful."

You know what gratitude does? It suffocates greed. When you're struggling with greed—when you're struggling with thinking, "Man, I need more. I'm not going to be happy unless I have the same car that my neighbors have," or "I'm not going to be happy unless I hit this number in my bank account," or "I'm not going to be happy until this, this, and this"— what is that? That's us creeping into discontent.

Discontent is the head of the snake of the spirit of mammon. But when you can be grateful, you're like, "You know what? If I had that thing, that'd be cool. But if I didn't have that thing, I'd still be good because I got what I need. I'm grateful. I'm grateful for what God is doing. I don't need more. I'm content."

Stomp. Serpent crushed.

## You Don't Need More to Be Content

I've seen this in my life personally, and I've seen testimony after testimony. It is one of the most consistent patterns I've observed, which to me indicates that it is absolutely a law in the kingdom of God: God is not motivated to give you something if you need to have it.

If you *need* to have that new car, if you *need* to have that new watch, if you *need* to have that boyfriend or that girlfriend—thinking, "Oh, I'm not going to be complete until I have that thing"—God will actually protect you from that thing because He doesn't want that thing to overtake you.

If you're not solidified and settled in your identity in Christ and in what He's given you, God doesn't want to compromise you. God doesn't want to give you a loaded gun and say, "You might shoot yourself with this, but hey, let's give it a shot." No. God wants to protect you.

I have seen over and over again that when God brings me to a place where I'm like, "Yeah, you know what? I don't need that thing. I just don't. I don't even really desire it," then God's like, "Perfect. Now I can trust you with it." Then God gives you these things, and you're like, "I didn't really need that, but that's awesome. Thank You. I really appreciate it, God. Thank You."

That is such a freeing place to live. Because what is that? That is you not serving money or things or possessions, but things are serving you as you serve God and the mission He has for you. That's the posture of contentment. That's the kind of heart God can bless.

## Don't Despise Small Beginnings

*For who has despised the day of small things?*

—Zechariah 4:10

Don't despise the day of small beginnings. Praise God for it. Praise God for what He's doing. There will be a day when you look back at where you're at right now, and you'll think, "Man, those were the good old days." Because increase also brings problems. It can increase headaches. You're increasing stewardship.

I love having four kids. It's way better than having one kid. But I'll tell you what: Our house is a lot messier with four kids than it was with one kid. Increase is a blessing, but increase also can be messy.

That's why the Bible says not to despise small beginnings. Because if you can't appreciate what God is doing in the small, how are you going to handle what He wants to give you later? That's the problem for a lot of people. They want God to give them more, but they're ungrateful for what's already in front of them. They're complaining about their current season instead of sowing in it. They're frustrated instead of faithful.

You've got to learn to look around and say, "God, thank You. I don't have everything I want, but I've got everything I need. And I trust You to grow this in Your time." That's how you steward the day of small things. That's how you show God you're ready for more.

## Contentment Prepares You for More

That's why it's so important to not rush past the season you're in. There are things God is building in you now that you're going to need later. Increase brings more responsibility, more moving parts, more pressure. It's all part of the package.

Don't despise the day of small beginnings. Be grateful for where you are, and God can entrust you with more later on. Gratitude isn't just a posture of faith; it's preparation. Because when you're content with where God has you, you're actually showing Him that you're ready to handle more. You're proving that you don't idolize increase, that you don't need the next thing to feel fulfilled, that you trust Him right where you are.

That's what God is looking for. Not striving. Not complaining. Not constantly reaching for what's next while ignoring what's already in your hands. He's looking for people who know how to stop, breathe, and say, "Thank You"; people who know how to be faithful with a little; people who can be trusted to carry more because they didn't resent what came before it.

When you get to that place, when you can live content, joyful, and grateful regardless of what season you're in, then God says, "Now you're ready." That's when you step into the kind of prosperity that's safe because it's rooted in trust.

It's not that you stopped wanting more. It's that you stopped needing more to feel whole. You found peace in the present. You found joy in the small. And you found out that the God who provides is also the God who protects you from what you're not ready for.

That's the posture He can bless. That's the heart He can increase. That's the mindset that prepares you for overflow.

That's the law of contentment.

## REFLECTION QUESTIONS

1. What blessings in your current season have you stopped celebrating?

2. How has discontentment blocked the flow of gratitude and generosity?

3. How can contentment position you for sustainable wealth?

Pray this out loud:

*Lord, thank You for what I already have. Guard my heart from greed and comparison. Teach me to rejoice in every stage of provision and to steward it well. I choose peace over pressure and gratitude over grasping. In Jesus' name, amen.*

To access additional resources, scan the QR code or visit thepowertoprosperbook. com/resources.

# CHAPTER 23

# THE LAW OF ENJOYMENT

WHEN THE ISRAELITES were finally free from Egypt, God didn't just lead them to battle. He led them into feasting. One of the first things He instituted in their national life was a calendar filled with celebrations: Passover, Pentecost, the Feast of Tabernacles. These weren't optional; they were commands. God literally *commanded* His people to stop, rest, enjoy food, enjoy drink, and rejoice in His blessing. Say it with me: He commanded His people *to party*!

Why? Because He knew the human heart is wired for worship. When we don't pause to enjoy what He's given, we start believing we earned it ourselves. Enjoyment is not selfish. It's spiritual.

But religion hates that idea. Religion wants you burned out, worn out, and convinced that suffering equals holiness. That's not the gospel. God gives good gifts, and He expects His people to actually enjoy them. When you refuse to enjoy what He's provided, you're not honoring Him; you're insulting Him. You're rejecting His generosity and pretending He's a hard master instead of a good Father.

Celebration matters. Joy matters. Rest, laughter, meals, and memories matter.

This is the law of enjoyment.

## Work Your Tail Off. Kick Your Feet Up.

What my pastor, Todd Doxzon, always says is, "Work your tail off; kick your feet up." Work hard. Play hard. Work really hard, then have fun. Celebrate. Throw a party. Go on vacation. Go to the movies. Go live life. Go enjoy the fruits of your labor.

Religious people hate this approach. They insist everything needs to be a sacrifice, everything needs to be painful. "You can't have fun with God," they say. But that's wrong. You should have fun with God. You should enjoy the life He's given you.

Take a look at Proverbs 10:16 (NLT):

> The earnings of the godly enhance their lives, but evil people squander
> their money on sin.

Do you hear that? The earnings of the godly enhance their lives. They make your life better. Get some new clothes. Upgrade your kitchen. Get a better fridge. Your car won't pass registration? Get a new vehicle. The earnings of the godly are meant to enhance your life. Use them with wisdom and moderation.

This isn't selfish; it's scriptural. God doesn't reward you so you can stay miserable. He blesses you so you can live, take care of the people you love, rest, reflect, laugh, and enjoy what you've worked for. You don't need to feel guilty about it. You need to feel grateful. Because this is what the blessing is for: not just to sow, not just to save, but to enjoy.

If that bothers your theology, wait until you see what Ecclesiastes has to say about it!

## It Is the Gift of God

> And also that every man should eat and drink and enjoy the good of
> all his labor—it is the gift of God.
>
> —ECCLESIASTES 3:13

Did you catch that? Enjoying the fruits of your labor *is a gift from God*. If you don't stop to enjoy what you've worked for, you're missing out on His gift. Here's the full context:

> I have seen the God-given task with which the sons of men are to be
> occupied. He has made everything beautiful in its time. Also He has
> put eternity in their hearts, except that no one can find out the work
> that God does from beginning to end. I know that nothing is better
> for them than to rejoice, and to do good in their lives, and also that
> every man should eat and drink and enjoy the good of all his labor—
> it is the gift of God.
>
> —ECCLESIASTES 3:10–13

That's not flesh. That's not compromise. That's the Bible speaking through Solomon by the Holy Spirit.

If you don't stop to enjoy what God has given you, you're rejecting a gift He meant for you to receive. It's not about materialism; it's about *trust*. It's about *not* living like a slave. It's about saying, "God, You've brought me here. You've blessed this. And now I'm going to stop and enjoy it."

Consider another passage from Ecclesiastes:

> Here is what I have seen: It is good and fitting for one to eat and drink, and to enjoy the good of all his labor in which he toils under the sun all the days of his life which God gives him; for it is his heritage. As for every man to whom God has given riches and wealth, and given him power to eat of it, to receive his heritage and rejoice in his labor—this is the gift of God.
>
> —ECCLESIASTES 5:18–19

God is a rewarder by nature. He loves to give good gifts to His children. So when you work with diligence, serve with faithfulness, and obey Him by stepping into your calling, He's not just going to give you provision. He's going to give you permission to enjoy it.

This doesn't mean living recklessly or spending everything you have. It means pausing to honor the moment and rejoicing in what God has done. When you understand that enjoyment is part of stewardship, it changes how you see your blessings and prepares you for more.

## You Should Have Fun with God

The Bible is clear: Enjoying life is the gift of God. The earnings of the godly enhance their lives. He "gives us richly all things to enjoy" (1 Tim. 6:17). Yet there are still people in the church who are offended by enjoyment, who can't wrap their heads around the idea that God actually wants His children to have fun.

It seems like most traditionalists despise this concept. They insist everything must be a sacrifice, everything must be painful in order for it to please God. But that's not true. You should have fun with God. That's what the Bible teaches and what He modeled throughout Scripture. From festivals to feasts, from rest to rejoicing, God built enjoyment into the rhythm of life.

Stop acting like enjoyment is something you have to apologize for. If you've been faithful, honored the Lord, and worked your tail off, it's time to kick your feet up. That's not carnal; that's biblical. That's covenantal!

If you don't stop and enjoy what God has done, you'll start worshipping the grind. You'll start thinking the work is the reward. You'll start believing that the only way to be spiritual is to be exhausted. And that's a lie.

Work your tail off; kick your feet up. I'll keep saying it because it's truth.

## The Religious Spirit Hates This

The religious crowd hates this truth. They're the ones who say, "Oh, you should live in a tent. You should make clothes out of sandpaper. That's how you'll honor the Lord with your life." It's crazy thinking that discomfort equals holiness. We have this warped theology where pain is equated with piety and blessing is treated like a curse.

But the Word of God doesn't say that.

> Command those who are rich in this present age not to be haughty, nor to trust in uncertain riches but in the living God, who gives us richly all things to enjoy.
>
> —1 TIMOTHY 6:17

God gives us richly all things to enjoy. Not to hoard. Not to worship. Not to find our identity in. But to enjoy, to receive, to use with gratitude. That's what the Bible says. Yet there are still people who would rather twist Scripture than admit they're offended by joy.

"Oh, that's all worldly. It's demonic. You should suffer. You should be poor. You should look miserable all the time." That's not spiritual; that's religious. That's flesh parading as holiness.

God gives us richly all things to enjoy. Let that sink in.

## Jesus Wasn't Against Enjoyment

Jesus wasn't against enjoyment. In fact, some of the religious people in His day were mad at Him because He was enjoying life. They said, "Look at this guy—He's eating with sinners. He's drinking. He's spending time at parties." They were offended because their view of righteousness was rooted in restriction. Their version of holiness was joyless.

But Jesus wasn't like that. He said, "The Son of Man came eating and drinking" (Matt. 11:19). Jesus knew how to celebrate. He showed up at weddings. He broke bread with people. He let a woman pour expensive oil on His feet and received it. He didn't say, "Oh no, don't waste that. That money could've been given to the poor." Someone else said that—Judas said that. Judas rebuked the offering, and Jesus corrected him.

Jesus understood value. He understood moments. He understood honor. He wasn't afraid of enjoyment or blessing. He didn't push it away when it was offered with a pure heart.

Yet people still want to act like joy is a distraction from holiness. They want to treat enjoyment like a temptation instead of a testimony. But when you understand what Jesus modeled, you stop listening to the critics. You stop pretending that righteousness and celebration are enemies. Because Jesus wasn't ashamed to enjoy what His Father provided—and we shouldn't be either.

Obviously, there's a difference between enjoyment and excess, but let me show you what happens when you actually learn how to receive blessing without guilt.

## Receiving Without Guilt

One of the best parts about being a father is blessing my kids with gifts. Whether it's gifting my son a new Lego set or taking my daughter out on a date, there's something that lights up inside me when I see them enjoying what I've given them or purchased for them.

But can you imagine how I would feel if I presented a special gift for them to enjoy, and either they didn't open it out of fear of appearing selfish, or they opened the gift, used the gift, but didn't dare give me any hint of enjoying it? How do you think that would make me as a father feel? Yet this is exactly how we make God the Father feel every time He blesses us and we don't fully receive what He's freely given us.

It seems painfully obvious when we reframe the situation as earthly parents with our earthly kids, but it's exactly how Jesus told us to relate to the Father when He exhorted His disciples, "If you, being evil parents, wouldn't give your kids a scorpion if they asked for an egg, how much more does the heavenly Father give good gifts to His children?" (Luke 11:12–13, paraphrased).

Asking for and gratefully receiving blessings from God is not carnal or worldly; it's worship! When you can look at what God has given you and say, "Thank You," that's the kind of heart He wants to bless. When you reach a place where you're not ashamed of the blessing—where you're not looking over your shoulder, waiting for someone to question your motives or accuse you of excess—you'll finally be able to receive what God wants to give without guilt.

This law isn't about indulgence; it's about freedom. Freedom from shame. Freedom from religion. Freedom from the pressure to downplay God's generosity so people don't get offended. God is the One who gives, and if He gives it, we can receive it.

> Every good gift and every perfect gift is from above, and comes down from the Father of lights.
>
> —JAMES 1:17

You don't need to apologize for the gifts. You don't need to hide what He's done in your life. You don't need to explain away every good thing. Just be faithful. Just be grateful. Just keep pointing the glory back to Him.

When you know how to receive blessing the right way, you're ready to handle more. You're ready to steward it with purity. You're ready to walk in it without letting it walk all over you.

And that brings us to the real question: Can you enjoy the blessing without letting it become your god?

This one's going to make all the religious people so mad. And I love it. Because God wants to reward you. That's who He is. God doesn't just bless your grind; He blesses your joy. He gives you richly all things to enjoy.

That means He wants you to enjoy your food, your rest, your time with your kids, the house He gave you—the reward of your labor. You don't need to apologize for it. You need to receive it like the gift that it is.

So go to dinner. Go on a trip. Go laugh until your stomach hurts. Go throw a party. Go make a memory. Because the blessing of God isn't just for stewardship; *it's for your enjoyment.* And when you receive it with a grateful heart, when you honor God with your rest as much as your work, you're walking in this truth.

That's the law of enjoyment.

# REFLECTION QUESTIONS

1. Where do you need to give yourself permission to enjoy what God has provided?

2. How could celebration become a form of worship in your financial life?

3. What does "resting in the blessing" look like for you right now?

Pray this out loud:

*Father, You delight in blessing Your children. Help me receive Your gifts with joy and rest, not guilt. Let my enjoyment be worship, reflecting that prosperity from You is holy and good. In Jesus' name, amen.*

To access additional resources, scan the QR code or visit thepowertoprosperbook.com/resources.

# CHAPTER 24

# THE LAW OF MINISTRY

THERE'S A COUPLE I know whose story marked me for life. They served in full-time ministry for decades, planting churches, preaching the gospel, and discipling the local church in small-town Pennsylvania. They weren't chasing fame or building platforms. They were building people.

Because of that commitment, they made real sacrifices. They never built wealth, didn't stockpile a retirement fund, and never strategized for a comfortable future. They just gave everything they had to the kingdom. When they finally reached retirement with no nest egg to rely on, something miraculous happened.

They discovered the land their house was built on contained oil. Literal oil. Rich reserves had been hidden under their feet the entire time. After they retired, the Lord allowed them to discover it. They received so much money from the oil rights that they never had to worry about money again.

It was like God waited until they were finished with their assignment, then said, "Now let Me take care of you." That's how He works. That's how He honors those who honor Him. That's what the law of ministry looks like in real life.

God never forgets those who serve His flock. When you make His people your priority, He makes your provision His. This isn't just a feel-good story that God will randomly do for some. This is a kingdom law. When you understand it, you stop chasing provision and start pursuing your assignment. Provision always follows purpose, especially when you're doing the work of ministry.

Let's talk about the law of ministry.

## Ministry Is Not a Pathway to Poverty

There's a lie that gets passed around in the church like it's biblical truth: Saying yes to ministry means saying yes to lack. If you go all in on what God's calling you to do, you'll have to settle for less money, less stability, less provision. Preaching the gospel means you're destined to live broke, burned-out, and barely getting by.

I believed that lie for a long time. I thought stepping into ministry meant sacrificing financial security. I liked nice things and still do. I liked being able to provide for my wife and kids, take them on trips, give to others, and not check the bank account before going out to dinner. I thought if I gave myself fully to ministry, all that would disappear. I thought I'd have to choose between doing what God called me to do and taking care of my family.

But I've learned something since then. Ministry isn't the road to lack but the road to *provision*. It's not the curse of scarcity but the call to overflow. I didn't figure that out by reading a book. I figured it out by obeying God.

When I laid down my business to focus on the ministry He was asking me to build, everything shifted. I had tried the other way, using my business to fund the ministry. But God wouldn't bless it. The moment I flipped it and stopped looking at ministry as something I'd fund later and started treating it like the thing I was *called* to steward now, provision showed up. Clients showed up. Resources showed up. But more importantly, peace showed up.

It wasn't because I was chasing money or gaming the system or pulling a prosperity lever. It was because I finally obeyed. That obedience unlocked a flow of financial favor I never experienced before in business. That's how the law of ministry works.

Jesus said it plainly:

> But seek first the kingdom of God and His righteousness, and all these things shall be added to you.
>
> —Matthew 6:33

*All these things.* Not just peace or wisdom. Your housing, food, clothing. The stuff most people spend their whole lives chasing. Jesus said to stop chasing it and start chasing Him. If you do, He'll make sure everything else is added to you.

But most people flip the order. They say, "Let me get these things in place first, then I'll serve the kingdom. Let me get my finances set, build this business, get my retirement secure. Then I'll answer the call." They wonder why nothing multiplies.

It's not that God doesn't want to bless them. He won't bless disobedience.

Partial obedience is still disobedience, and delayed obedience is really just disbelief in disguise.

So many people try to play it safe financially before saying yes to ministry. But there's nothing safe about disobeying God. The safest place you can be is in full surrender. When you step into your assignment, you don't have to *make* it work because God already has. He funds what He initiates. He provides for what He ordains. When you get serious about your kingdom assignment, He gets serious about resourcing you.

I had been treating ministry like a side hustle, something I could get to once my business was big enough. But God flipped the whole script. He said, "Your ministry doesn't need your business to be successful. Your business needs your ministry to be successful." When I got that revelation and obeyed it, everything changed.

Jesus doesn't call us to struggle through ministry hoping someone will bail us out. He calls us to serve, then promises to back that service with supernatural supply. You want to live in overflow? Stop waiting for the stars to align, for the bank account to look right, for someone to sponsor your calling. Say yes now. Ministry isn't the path to poverty but the path to God's provision.

And that's just the beginning.

## God Pays His Laborers

Let me ask you a serious question: If Jesus promised you a paycheck, would you believe Him?

Because *He did*. I'm not just talking about some spiritual reward you'll cash in when you get to heaven. That's real, yes. But Jesus promised something for now. Real wages. Real provision for those who labor in the ministry, for those who say yes to their kingdom assignments not just in theory but in full surrender.

This goes against what many of us were taught. Somewhere along the way, the church got this twisted idea that full-time ministry should come with full-time struggle. If you're really in it for God, you'll prove it by staying poor. You'll live on fumes, beg for scraps, and store up "treasures in heaven" by forfeiting everything here on earth (Matt. 6:20). But that's not what Jesus taught, not what Paul modeled, and not what I've seen in my life.

> And he who reaps receives wages, and gathers fruit for eternal life, that both he who sows and he who reaps may rejoice together.
>
> —John 4:36

Let that hit you. "He who reaps receives wages." Not just favor or spiritual goose bumps. *Wages.* Provision. Pay. That's Jesus talking, describing a very real principle in the kingdom of God: If you do the work of ministry, God will make sure you're taken care of.

It's not hype or prosperity gospel nonsense. It's a law. I didn't always believe it.

I've shared this in part, but when I was still building my business, trying to keep ministry on the side, I was stuck in fear. I thought, "If I go all in with ministry, who's going to take care of me? Who's going to pay the bills? How will I survive?" I was working hard, chasing clients, hustling to build a digital media agency—but it just wasn't working. Everything felt hard, like I was fighting the wind.

Then one day, God asked me something that wrecked me. He said, "Kap, would you let *Me* be your only client?"

I froze. Deep down I didn't believe that I would. I believed He was good, just not that good. I believed He'd provide, but not like *that*. I believed in His promises, but I didn't trust Him enough to lay everything else down. I wanted a backup plan, something safe.

But He was inviting me into *trust*.

When I finally said yes to that question and told Him, "OK, Lord, You be my only client. I'll preach what You tell me to preach, make the content You want me to make, build what You tell me to build, and trust You with the outcome," everything changed.

I didn't have to beg, manipulate, or squeeze money out of people. I just had to obey. God started moving.

> The laborer is worthy of his wages.
>
> —Luke 10:7

When Jesus sent out His disciples, He told them not to take a bag or extra money, or to have a fallback plan. Just go. Preach. Heal. Minister. Trust that God will provide.

And God did—through people, homes, meals, divine appointments.

God made sure His workers were taken care of because He always takes care of His own.

Paul knew this. He said,

> If we have sown spiritual things for you, is it a great thing if we reap your material things?
>
> —1 CORINTHIANS 9:11

This isn't about greed or entitlement but about *order*. When you sow spiritually, when you give yourself to the work of the Word, it's not only right but *righteous* to receive material provision in return.

Paul took it even further:

> Let the elders who rule well be counted worthy of double honor, especially those who labor in the word and doctrine.
>
> —1 TIMOTHY 5:17

*Double* honor. That's not just a pat on the back but support, provision, partnership. It's a biblical pattern: Those who give themselves to full-time ministry should be able to do it full-time without worrying about how they're going to feed their kids or pay their rent.

This isn't new. Jesus Himself was funded by people who believed in what He was doing:

> And many others...provided for Him from their substance.
>
> —LUKE 8:3

People think Jesus was broke. But Scripture shows us He was supported by women, families, and those who saw the power of His ministry and wanted to be part of it. He didn't reject it but received it because He knew it wasn't just generosity but honor.

Honor fuels ministry. When you give your life to ministry, you don't need to beg for help because God will put it on people's hearts to help you. He'll send the ravens, touch the widow's house, and move through your audience, clients, supporters, and partners. He'll do it however He wants to, but He will provide.

If He calls you, He'll cover you. If He sends you, He'll supply you.

You're not trusting in people, platforms, or your ability to sell merch or create revenue streams or build funnels. You're trusting in the One who said,

> Seek first the kingdom of God...and all these things will be added to you.
>
> —Matthew 6:33, esv

And He meant it.

You don't need a hundred clients. You just need one. If God is your only client, you'll never lack a thing.

## Ministry Is a Two-Way Covenant

There are zero scriptures in the entire Bible about how to beg other people for money. However, there are over two thousand verses that instruct and testify and mandate that the people of God help other people come out of poverty.[1] This is the heart of God. The heart of God is not to keep people in poverty but to lift people out of poverty. We know this because God promises it consistently and mandates us to do the same.

It's a lot like flying on an airplane. Have you ever flown on an airplane and seen the flight attendants go through all the safety checks? They teach you where the life jackets are, where the emergency exits are. What do they always say about what happens when the oxygen masks come down? They say, "Put your oxygen mask on first if you're next to a child, and then put your child's oxygen mask on."

The parallel I'm making is not that you should be selfish before being selfless. The parallel is that you can do a lot more good for people around you when you get your life figured out first. When you get this area of your life figured out first, giving becomes a lot easier. You know, "OK, I've got the systems. I understand God's laws and principles and promises in this area of my life so that I can be just a river for resources to flow through, to meet needs, to accelerate the advancement of the gospel."

God's design is not one-sided. It's not just about ministers pouring out without ever receiving. It's also not just about people giving without receiving spiritual nourishment. It's a covenant. Ministry is a two-way covenant. When both sides honor the covenant, God moves. The laborer is taken care of, and the people are blessed. The kingdom advances.

This is the model we see throughout Scripture. Elijah didn't manipulate the widow or guilt her into giving her last meal. He simply spoke the word of the Lord. She responded in faith. When she did, her house never lacked. That's the beauty of this covenant. Both the minister and the recipient get blessed. Both are part of the miracle.

That's how God set it up. That's why you don't have to beg or plead or manipulate when you're doing God's work. Just obey. Just speak what He tells you to say. Just do what He tells you to do. Because when you're aligned with His assignment, He'll bring the provision through people who are just as hungry for breakthrough as you are to deliver it.

## Your Business Needs Your Ministry— Not the Other Way Around

I have to come full circle, back to what I was talking about with my ministry. When I'd been successful in one thing, I thought, "Oh, I can just do it this way, the way that I've been doing it. We'll just kind of coast off into the sunset, and it'll be good." So God had to really pull the rug from underneath me as I went into 2025.

He was like, "Kap, you're getting way too comfortable, man. You're doing all these reaction videos—that's cool. You're reaching the lost. But you're not making disciples to the degree that I want you to." He said, "People are getting saved. People are watching these videos. You're getting views. You're gaining more subscribers. But then what? What are you going to do with the people who give their lives to Jesus? What are you going to do with the people who don't have a church? What are you going to do with *them?*"

Then He challenged me even deeper.

"Or is this just about metrics now? Are you just stroking your ego, collecting a paycheck from the YouTube ad revenue? Is that really what you want? Or are you going to care about souls? Are you about *My* business? Or are you building *your* brand?"

Coming into 2025, the Lord had to purify my heart. That's why for the first couple of months, from December through February and into March, I pulled back. I hardly posted any reaction videos. The numbers started dropping. Views were down. Subscribers left. Ad revenue took a dive.

But I had to go through that for this purpose. I had to go through that because the Lord said, "Kap, it is time to expand. It's time to build this ministry to house all the descendants"—just like Isaiah 54 says.

He laid it out clearly: "I want you to build an addition. I want you to invest in a new studio. I want you to get serious about the podcast *Directed Life*."

Then He made it plain: "Kap, this is expansion season. It's time for you to start coaching people, time to start taking multiplication seriously, time to build up others who will do what you're doing."

All this—every new structure, every investment—was for one thing: to better care for the people He already sent.

God said, "Why would I send more if you're not taking care of the ones I've already entrusted to you? Why would I give you more souls if you're not feeding the sheep?" That hit hard. "He who is faithful with little will be entrusted with much more."

I caught the vision. I said to God, "I can't hold back."

New equipment. Four cameras. Studio furniture. Hiring staff. Investing in software. Running ads. Sparing no expense.

Why?

Because of the law of ministry.

How could God entrust me with more if I wasn't being faithful with what He'd already placed in my hands?

Most people would look at what we're doing and say, "That's crazy. All that investment?" But it's for eternal purposes. So as I write, I know God's going to bless it. He's done it before. Over and over again. And He'll do it again.

## Stop Making Excuses—Start Obeying

You might be in a season right now when you're giving it everything you've got. You're doing everything you can, trying to be faithful. You're grinding, staying up late, showing up early, hustling every day, and still you're not seeing breakthrough. You're not seeing the fruit. You feel like you're doing everything right, but it's not working. You're asking, "What more can I do?"

That's literally what Peter was going through with his fishing business. He had worked all night, done everything he knew to do. He had used all his experience, all his skill, all his effort. And he still came up empty.

> Master, we have toiled all night and caught nothing.
>
> —LUKE 5:5

But then Peter said something that changed everything. He said, "Nevertheless at Your word I will let down the net" (Luke 5:5).

That word *nevertheless* might be the most powerful word you can speak when you're exhausted, discouraged, or confused. It's the word that bridges the gap between frustration and faith. Peter was saying, "Lord, I don't see it. I don't feel it. I don't even think it's going to work. But because You said it, I'll do it." That's what obedience looks like. It's not obeying when it makes sense but obeying when it doesn't.

Peter was basically thinking, "This guy has no business telling me what to do. He's never fished a day in His life. I've been doing this my whole life. But what else am I going to do? I might as well just do what He's saying." When he did, and when he obeyed, he caught a great number of fish. A supernatural number. So many fish that his nets started to break. It was the biggest catch he had ever seen. And that wasn't even the most miraculous part.

Can I tell you something? The first miracle Peter ever experienced Jesus do wasn't casting out a demon, healing a sick person, or calming a storm. It was this: Jesus blessed his business. Jesus stepped into his workplace, spoke a word, and brought increase.

That's how Peter became a disciple. That's how he decided to follow Jesus. He saw that Jesus cared about his work, his livelihood, his provision. So when people say business doesn't matter to God, that God cares only about spiritual things, or that material increase is ungodly, take it up with Jesus. Because it was business breakthrough that made Peter a believer.

"And their net was breaking" (Luke 5:6). The blessing was so overwhelming that the system they were using couldn't even contain it. It was too much. So what did they do? They signaled to their partners in the other boat to come and help them. The other boat came, and even that boat started to sink because of how great the increase was.

Peter was being blessed by God so much that he had to call others to it. "Come get a piece of this. There's too much. I can't carry this by myself." Now that other boat, those other fishermen, got to be a part of the harvest too.

That's how the kingdom works. Don't think small. Don't play it safe. Don't limit your assignment to what you think you can handle. Think big with God. Step out in faith. Stop making excuses and start obeying. Because the blessing you're believing for might be on the other side of that one word: *nevertheless*.

## You're Not Called to Survive—
## You're Called to Serve

Ministry is not a pathway to poverty. In fact, dogged commitment to ministry has a law behind it that accelerates the financial anointing in your life.

Again, my story personally: I was doing business, building a digital media agency, and helping pastor a church, but as a volunteer. As I've mentioned, I thought, "Once I build the business to a place of success, then I'll be able to focus on ministry."

God had to bring me to this place of realization: "Kap, if you would just get focused on winning souls. If you would just get focused on preaching the Word of God. If you would just get focused on reaching your generation with the Word. Will you trust, Kap, that I'm a better boss than anybody in the world could be? Are you willing to trust, Kap, that I'm a better client than anybody in the world could be? I'm just looking for someone to trust Me and go all in with what I'm telling them to do."

I said, "God, I want to. I want to believe that. But I just don't believe it's going to work out for me in the end." I kid you not.

I stepped into ministry not to make a profit but out of obedience because nothing else was working. I said, "God, I have nowhere else to go. I'm going to say yes. I'm going to say a wholehearted yes to what You're telling me to do. I'm going all in on my ministry."

And here's what happened: That year, the reward—for me, for my family, and for the ministry—was greater than anything I'd ever experienced in business. Ever. Not because I got lucky or because God likes me more than anyone else. It was the result of a spiritual law I had glossed over and ignored in Scripture. It's all over the place. God is simply looking for people who will say, "I believe You, Father. I'm willing to go all in. I'm not going to worry about money. I'm going to focus on what You care about—souls—and I'll trust You with the rest."

And let me tell you, God takes care of the rest better than you ever could.

This is the law of ministry: When you go all in on God's assignment, He goes all in on your provision. When you stop treating ministry like a side hustle and start treating it like your mandate, heaven responds. Souls get saved. Needs get met. God gets glory.

You don't have to survive doing what He called you to do. You get to thrive doing it. You don't need everyone to understand it or support it. You just need to say yes. If you do, the same God who sent you will be the same God who sustains you. Every single time.

That's the law of ministry.

## REFLECTION QUESTIONS

1. What assignment has God called you to build that could bless others and generate provision?

2. How can you let ministry lead and allow money to follow?

3. Where is God asking you to trust Him as your only source of support?

Pray this out loud:

*Jesus, I dedicate my gifts, income, and influence to Your mission. You are my provider and my reward. Use my obedience to fund revival, transform lives, and expand Your kingdom through me. In Jesus' name, amen.*

To access additional resources, scan the QR code or visit thepowertoprosperbook. com/resources.

# PART IV

# THE PURPOSE OF PROSPERITY

## CHAPTER 25

# BUILDING A LEGACY THAT OUTLIVES YOU

IF YOU WANT to prosper well and stand against the spirit of mammon in these last days, you need to build a legacy that outlives you. Make a decision that your life and your resources are not your own. You are a steward, and you're going to move that resource where your Father says to move it so you can fulfill your assignment on the earth.

Again, Paul told Timothy,

> Command those who are rich in this present age not to be haughty, nor to trust in uncertain riches but in the living God, who gives us richly all things to enjoy. Let them do good, that they be rich in good works, ready to give, willing to share, storing up for themselves a good foundation for the time to come, that they may lay hold on eternal life.
>
> —1 TIMOTHY 6:17–19

That's the picture. Prosper well. Steward well. Think beyond your own comfort, and consider eternity. Think about the people God called you to bless and the legacy you'll leave behind when your time on earth is done. Building a legacy doesn't start with saving; it starts with sowing.

## Legacy Starts with Generosity

If you want to build a legacy that matters, you have to start with generosity. Not strategy, not branding, but generosity. This is how you break the spirit of mammon off your life. This is how you tell money, "You don't own me." This is how you align yourself with the heart of God.

Having money isn't wrong, but when money has *you*, that's the issue. The number one way to break that grip is through sacrifice.

The Bible is clear: Honor the Lord with your possessions and with the firstfruits of all your increase. Why? Not because God needs your money but because God wants your *heart*. "Where your treasure is, there your heart will be also" (Matt. 6:21). Every time you tithe, give an offering, respond to a need, or sow into the kingdom, you're making a statement in the spirit: "I don't serve money. Money serves me as I serve God."

Whether you have a little or a lot, the temptation is the same. When you don't think God can meet your needs, you'll try to hold on to what you have. That's how mammon creeps in. But every time you give when it's uncomfortable, when it stretches you, when it costs you, that's when legacy begins. You're not just giving to be generous. You're giving to break the cycle and build something bigger than you.

## Giving Hurts Mammon—and Heals You

Here's how you shut down the spirit of mammon: You don't argue with it or pray it away. You *give*. Every time you feel that resistance in your heart—the hesitation to tithe, the reluctance to cover the bill, that inner cringe when someone brings up generosity—it's not just a budget issue. It's a spiritual opportunity. It's a chance to say, "I'm not going to serve money. I'm going to serve God *with* my money."

Sometimes giving should stretch you. It should challenge you and cost you. If your giving never requires faith, then you're probably giving in comfort, and comfort never breaks mammon. When you give what hurts, when you give what you could have kept, when you give what you thought you needed, *that's when your heart shifts*. Fear loses its grip. The enemy backs off because you've chosen worship over worry.

David said it best: "I will not offer to the LORD...sacrifices that cost me nothing" (2 Sam. 24:24, NET). That wasn't religious talk. That was a man who understood covenant. That was a man who understood what it means to give like God owns everything and to trust that He'll provide whatever is needed next.

When you give like that, you won't just experience personal freedom. You'll see that real prosperity was never supposed to stop with you in the first place.

## Prosperity That Doesn't Spill Over Isn't Prosperity

When you give what costs you something, when you worship God with your finances instead of letting money dictate your decisions, something happens. Not just in your heart but in your hands. You realize that real prosperity was never meant to stop with you.

God's goal isn't just to meet your needs. He cares about that, yes. He wants your kids to have braces. He wants you to date your spouse and take your family on vacation. But He also wants you to have more than enough—not just so you can live in comfort but so you can meet every occasion to be generous.

The Bible says that when you give, God will make all grace abound toward you, not so you can hoard it but so you'll have all sufficiency in all things and an abundance for every good work. That's the point of overflow. It's not to impress people. It's not to insulate your lifestyle. It's to build capacity to meet needs that aren't your own.

If everything God gives you terminates with you, that's not prosperity; it's spiritual constipation. Prosperity isn't just about your bills getting paid. It's about the people connected to you having their needs met too. It's about seeing increase and immediately asking, "God, who is this for?" When prosperity is redeemed, it multiplies beyond the bank account and changes lives.

When you start prospering like that, you better get ready. The blessing attracts the battle.

## If It Stops with You, It Dies with You

If all you're thinking about is how to make sure you're set up for success and maybe that your family's taken care of too, but you're not thinking about anyone else, you're not thinking big enough.

You're not thinking legacy. You're thinking survival.

That's not how God thinks. That's not how kingdom people build. When you think legacy, you start asking God, "Who else is supposed to come under this roof? Who else is supposed to be blessed by what I'm building? Who else is going to be lifted because I said yes?"

If the increase God gives you ends with you, that's not stewardship; it's self-preservation. If it stops with you, it dies with you.

But when you're faithful with what He puts in your hand, when you steward the vision and invite others into it, when you build something big enough to hold other people, you're not just prospering. You're multiplying. Consider how Peter's net-breaking miracle brought in other boats. When you build with God, *it spills onto others*.

Legacy isn't just about what you leave behind. It's about what you build that blesses people while you're still here.

## Think Beyond Your Lifetime

If you want to build a legacy, you can't just think about today, or even just think about your kids. You have to think about your kids' kids. As we've seen, one verse in Proverbs puts it this way:

> A good man leaves an inheritance to his children's children, but the wealth of the sinner is stored up for the righteous.
> —PROVERBS 13:22

That's legacy. That's God's definition of a righteous life: someone who builds beyond themselves, someone who sees what they've been given as a trust fund from heaven—not just for survival but for stewardship. A good man is thinking long-term and asking God, "How can I set up the next generation for success?"

You just have to be faithful. Do the best with what you have *now*. Steward what God has already placed in your hand. If you do, He'll give you more because God entrusts more to those who manage it well. Legacy grows not by being flashy but by being consistent, intentional, and generational.

When you think like that, when you take your eyes off just your own comfort, you'll realize something even greater: What God is building through you isn't just for your family. It's for others too.

## What You Build Should Bless Others

When you start thinking generationally, you realize that what God's doing in your life isn't just for your household. *It's for others too.* If all you're doing is building something for yourself and your immediate family, you're missing the bigger picture. Legacy is bigger than comfort and inheritance. It's about creating something others can walk into and be blessed by simply because you said yes.

God takes notice when you build like that, when you're thinking about others and not just yourself. He's not just looking at what you're building; He's watching who you're building it for.

## God Pays Those Who Build What He Cares About

As we've seen with the law of ministry, when you build what's in God's heart, He makes sure it's resourced. He doesn't let kingdom assignments go underfunded. If it's His vision, He'll provide the provision. And not just to get the job done but to bless you in the process. He's a rewarder.

Paul understood this. He said, "Not that I seek the gift, but I seek the fruit that abounds to your account" (Phil. 4:17). He wasn't begging or manipulating. He was confident. He knew that when people partner with what God is doing, *God keeps track.* There's fruit that gets credited to your account in heaven. Eternal reward. Lasting legacy. Paul said, "I have all and abound. I am full" (v. 18). Why? Because the church at Philippi didn't just hear about the mission. They invested in it. They gave faithfully. As a result, they shared in the fruit.

I've seen this too. As I've consecrated my business to God and committed to building what He told me to build, the presence of God has stayed on it. People who have come under that covering—whether as clients, team members, or partners—they've experienced miracles. We had team members who were unable to conceive for over a decade. After coming into partnership with what we were building, God opened the door. They got pregnant. I don't take the glory. I give it to God. But I've seen the pattern. When you build something God cares about, He breathes on it, and the blessing extends to everyone involved.

Legacy doesn't just come from what you *own.* It comes from what you *build* that blesses others. When you do that with eternity in mind, when you build with the harvest in your heart, God makes sure the resources keep flowing.

At the end of the day, legacy isn't just about how much you gave or what you built. It's about who you built it for.

## If You Take Care of His Kids, He'll Take Care of the Cash

This is what I believe God wants to say to you today: If you take care of My kids, I'll take care of the cash.

That's how He thinks. That's how His kingdom works. God is looking for people who will align their hearts with what He cares about most: *people.* Souls. Lives. The poor. The lost. The next generation. When you show Him that you're about His kids, He'll show you that He's about your needs.

The Bible says God owns the cattle on a thousand hills. The earth is His footstool. The streets of heaven are paved with gold. He's not short on resources. But what He's looking for is *trust.* He's looking for stewardship. He's looking for people who say, "God, if You'll get it to me, I'll get it to them." That's the kind of heart He can bless. That's the kind of heart that carries legacy.

You want to leave a mark on the earth? Take care of His people. Meet needs. Fund the gospel. Lift people out of poverty. Help feed and disciple the next generation. God doesn't forget the ones who remember His mission.

That's legacy. It's not just money in a will. It's fruit that follows you into eternity. It's a reward you get to enjoy *here* and *there.*

## This Is the Call to Build for Eternity

If you want to prosper well and stand against the spirit of mammon, you need to make a decision today that your life and your resources are not your own, that you're a steward. You're not building your own kingdom. You're building something that outlives you.

God entrusts increase because He's looking for people who think generationally, people who will look beyond their own comfort and even their children's comfort to consider the next generation—their grandchildren and people they'll never meet but whose lives will be shaped by the decisions they make today.

The Bible says, "Store up for yourselves treasures in heaven" (Matt. 6:20, NIV). God's wisdom through Proverbs declares you should be leaving an inheritance for your kids' kids (13:22). That means you should be asking, "God, how do I steward what You've given me to build something that lasts? Something that multiplies? Something that blesses others and gives You glory long after I'm gone?"

God is looking for legacy builders. He's looking for those who understand that wealth without worship is wasted. That increase without obedience is empty. That success without surrender is meaningless.

So take care of His kids. Take care of His mission. Take care of the resources He's put in your hands. And let Him take care of the rest.

To access additional resources, scan the QR code or visit thepowertoprosperbook. com/resources.

# CHAPTER 26

# CONTINUING IN GENEROSITY AND GIVING

ONE OF THE biggest traps people fall into when it comes to generosity is making it seasonal. They treat giving like it's a moment instead of a lifestyle. They tithe once, give a big offering once, then look at their bank accounts and say, "Well, nothing happened. I gave to God, and it didn't work."

Let me just say it plainly: When you say that, you're calling God a liar.

Either God is true or He's not. Either His Word is dependable or it's not. If He said that when you give, it will be given back to you—pressed down, shaken together, and running over—then the harvest is coming. If He said, "Honor the LORD with your possessions, and with the firstfruits of your increase; so your barns will be filled with plenty" (Prov. 3:9–10), then that's exactly what He means. And if He said we should "not grow weary in doing good, for in due season we shall reap, if we do not give up" (Gal. 6:9, MEV), then guess what? The only thing that can stop your harvest is giving up too soon.

But that's what many believers do. They treat sowing like a lottery ticket, giving once and expecting a miracle by morning. When it doesn't come in the form they expected, they say, "It didn't work."

This is not a game of chance. This is a covenant. This is a law. You will reap what you sow. That's not my opinion; that's the Word of God. When you give, you're activating that law. But like a farmer who plants a seed, you don't see the fruit the next day. You've got to water it, protect it, and keep showing up in faith day after day, even when you don't feel like it. The seed is working even if you can't see it.

Galatians 6:9 reminds us not to grow weary in doing good, "for in due season we shall reap if we do not lose heart." The key phrase? "In due season." There's a time for sowing and a time for reaping. There's a gap between obedience and overflow. But the promise is clear: *You will reap.*

The only people who don't reap are the ones who quit too early. The ones who get weary. The ones who accuse God of failing. The ones who let disappointment rewrite their theology. But when you stand your ground—when you stay faithful even in the drought, even in the silence, even when every voice around you says, "Why are you still giving?"—that's when heaven starts to move.

Giving can't be circumstantial. It can't be based on how good the worship was on Sunday or whether the preacher moved you. Your giving has to be based on covenant, consistency, and conviction. It has to be something you've resolved in your spirit to do no matter what the account balance says. When you make giving a lifestyle, you experience the lifestyle of the blessed.

You've heard me say this before, but it's worth repeating: The antidote to greed isn't just giving once. It's living a life of giving. Generosity isn't a one-time gesture; it's a declaration of allegiance. Every time you give, especially when it hurts, you are choosing sides. You declare, "I refuse to be ruled by the spirit of mammon. I serve the God who multiplies."

So keep giving. Keep sowing. Keep stretching. Keep releasing. Don't let your generosity be based on emotion or circumstance. Make it a rhythm, a value, a lifestyle. When you refuse to grow weary in doing good, when you keep your hand to the plow and your heart anchored in faith, the harvest will come, *in due season.*

## Greed Isn't Just for the Rich

When people hear the word *greed,* they picture Scrooge McDuck or some billionaire hoarding piles of cash. But the truth is, greed isn't limited to the wealthy. Greed has nothing to do with your bank account and everything to do with your heart. Some of the most tightfisted, stingy, and fear-driven people I've ever met weren't rich at all. They were broke. I say that not with condemnation but with compassion because I've been there.

When you have very little, the temptation to worship money gets louder, not quieter. Every dollar feels like it could slip away. You think, "I can't afford to give. I need to hold on to what I have." But that's exactly how the spirit of mammon traps you—through fear of lack. Whether you have much or little, the question isn't how much you possess. The question is, Who possesses you?

I've felt it. I've had those moments when the bank account was low, and I knew the right thing to do was to be generous, but everything in me said, "Not this time. Play it safe. Be responsible." But it wasn't wisdom speaking; it was fear. It was that whisper of mammon trying to convince me that my future depended on how tightly I held my money.

In those moments, you have to make a decision. You have to treat giving like warfare. As I've said, that's when you have to declare, "I don't serve money. Money serves me as I serve God."

Every time you tithe, every time you give, especially when it hurts, you're making a spiritual declaration. You're saying, "I'm not the source. God is." You're declaring, "Money doesn't rule me. Jesus does." When you give like that, when you stretch like that, when you step into ouch-offering territory, something breaks off you. The grip of mammon loses its hold, and your faith grows stronger than your fear.

Let me be clear: Having money doesn't make you greedy. Being broke doesn't make you holy. It's not about the size of your wallet—it's about the posture of your heart. If you let fear drive your financial decisions, you'll stay trapped in cycles of lack, no matter how much income you generate. But if you trust God enough to keep giving even in scarcity, He'll trust you enough to keep blessing you with abundance.

The spirit of greed doesn't wait for your income to increase. It shows up the moment you start thinking, "What I have isn't enough, and it never will be." But the Spirit of God invites you into a different mindset: "What I have came from Him, and I can trust Him to supply again."

## Every Act of Giving Is Spiritual Warfare

Most people don't realize it, but every time you give, you're stepping onto a battlefield. Giving isn't just a financial act; it's a spiritual act. It's warfare. Every offering, every tithe, every act of generosity you sow into the kingdom is an act of war against the spirit of mammon.

Mammon doesn't just want your money. Mammon wants your heart, your trust, your worship. Every time you release what's in your hand, especially when it stretches you, you're declaring mammon has no authority over you. You're saying, "I know where my help comes from. I know who my provider is. I refuse to be ruled by fear."

People think spiritual warfare is just about casting out demons or praying in tongues. Yes, that's part of it. But there's another kind of spiritual warfare most people overlook: radical obedience in your finances. When the enemy whispers, "You can't afford to give," and you give anyway—that's warfare. When you feel the pull to hoard, to self-protect, to wait for a better time—and instead you sow sacrificially—that's warfare.

Generosity is one of the clearest ways to expose the lies of the enemy. It breaks the back of scarcity, dethrones the idol of money, and declares, "My source is eternal. My supply doesn't come from this economy. I serve a God who multiplies."

The enemy hates that. He hates it because he knows what's on the other side of it. He knows that when you give with a pure heart, not only are you blessed but others are impacted. Souls are saved. Churches are funded. Ministries are launched. Needs are met. The kingdom of God advances.

That's why the enemy will fight you harder in this area than almost any other. If he can keep you fearful, he can keep you stuck. If he can keep you clenched, he can keep you ineffective. But the moment you open your hand, your heart opens too. That's when the miracle begins. That's when your seed starts breaking strongholds—not just in your life but in the lives of those you're giving to.

So don't just give casually. Give intentionally. Give prayerfully. Give with authority. Understand what's at stake, and understand the kind of power you're stepping into when you give. When you give to the things of God, you're not losing; you're launching. You're releasing God's power into your finances, your family, your future.

You're declaring war on the spirit of mammon.

And you're winning.

## The Power of the Ouch Offering

There's a type of giving that shifts things in the spirit. It's not casual, convenient, or automatic. It's costly. It stretches your faith, tests your trust, and pulls something deep out of you. I love how a pastor I know puts it: He calls it the *ouch offering*.

That phrase captures it perfectly. It's the kind of offering that makes your flesh wince. It's the kind of generosity that makes you stop and think,

"God, I really hope this is You asking for this." It's the kind that makes your knees buckle a little, not because you're afraid of losing something but because you're surrendering something that matters.

And that's exactly why it matters.

Again, David said it like this: "I will not offer to the LORD...sacrifices that cost me nothing" (2 Sam. 24:24, NET). That's reverence. That's real faith. That's what worship looks like in your bank account.

The *ouch offering* isn't just about dollars; it's about dependence. It's about reminding yourself who your source really is. It's about declaring out loud, in action, that money doesn't own you; God does. It's declaring that you don't live by spreadsheets; you live by obedience. You're not giving to impress anyone; you're giving to honor the One who gave everything for you.

I've had those moments. I've felt that internal war. I've stared at the number God told me to give and thought, "This doesn't make any sense." But I gave it anyway. Not out of emotion. Not out of manipulation. Out of raw trust. Time and time again, God has proved that He cannot be outgiven.

Here's what I've found: The greatest financial breakthroughs I've ever seen were always preceded by an ouch offering. Not a reckless offering. Not a manipulative offering. But a real one. A "God, I trust You more than I trust my cushion" kind of offering. That's when miracles happen. That's when strongholds break. That's when provision hits.

If you're wrestling with it right now, if you feel the nudge to give but your brain is fighting it, just remember this: Every time you choose generosity over greed, you're not just making a transaction. You're making a statement in the spirit realm. You're declaring war on mammon. You're taking ground back from fear. You're telling hell, "You don't own me anymore."

More importantly, you're telling God, "You can trust me."

It's not about how big the gift is; it's about the position of your heart. The ouch offering may empty your wallet for a moment, but it fills your life with what money can't buy: God's favor, God's presence, and God's supernatural provision.

So give when it hurts. Give when it stretches you. Give when it doesn't make sense. That's when God shows up.

# Giving Isn't a Gift to God—It's a Reminder to You

We have to stop thinking that when we give to God, we're doing Him a favor. God doesn't need your money. He's not short on cash. He's not looking at your tithe like it's rent for the month. He owns the cattle on a thousand hills. He owns the hills. He owns the earth. The silver is His. The gold is His. When you give, you're not adding to His supply; you're training your heart.

Giving isn't a gift to God. It's a reminder to you.

Every time I tithe, every time I sow, every time I pay for the check at lunch when I really wanted someone else to cover it, it's not just about the dollar amount. It's about what it does in me. It's a line in the sand that says, "I still remember where this came from." It's me telling my soul, "You don't serve money. You serve God. Money serves you as you serve Him."

That's why tithing is such a powerful practice. It's also why the enemy fights it so hard in the church. When you consistently give the first and best of your increase to God, you're building spiritual muscle memory. You're training yourself not to get comfortable, not to take credit, not to start leaning on the numbers. You're reminding yourself, "This belongs to Him. It always has."

Think about what it means to *consecrate* something—to consecrate your business, your platform, your family. That word means to set something apart, to say, "This is not mine to do with whatever I please. This is holy. This belongs to the Lord."

Giving is how you practice consecration with your income. It's how you say, "This isn't just cash flow. This isn't just revenue. This isn't just net profit. This is seed, and it's sacred."

When you live like that, when you make giving a rhythm, not a reaction, you don't just consecrate your money. You consecrate your mind, your motives, your methods. You keep yourself from drifting into mammon's territory because every act of generosity is an act of remembrance.

So when you write that check, when you transfer that money, when you sow into your church or into a ministry that's feeding you, don't just see it as a transaction. See it as a declaration. You're saying, "I remember. I trust You. I know where this came from, and I'm not going to forget who the source is."

## You Can't Sow Without Reaping

Let's go back to one of the most fundamental laws in all Scripture: the law of sowing and reaping. I've taught on this before in detail, but there's something we need to lock in here again—not just the promise of the law but the pattern of it. If you want to continue to reap, you have to continue to sow. This isn't just a onetime act of obedience; it's a lifestyle of alignment.

Think of a farmer again. He works his field, plants seed, waters it, and eventually reaps a harvest. But what happens if he says, "Well, I got what I needed. My barn's full. I'm done"? It might feel like a win at the moment, but he's just created a future crisis. When the supply runs out—and it always does—there won't be another harvest waiting. Why? Because he stopped sowing.

The same thing happens to believers all the time. We go through a season of generosity, God shows up, He blesses us, He increases us, and then we coast. We pause. We assume the harvest will just keep coming. But we forget the principle: If you stop sowing, you'll eventually stop reaping. Your barn might be full now, but it won't stay full forever.

Sowing isn't a crisis response. It's not something you pull out when you need God to rescue you. It's not an emergency button you hit when your account dips too low. It's a rhythm, a way of living, a declaration you make again and again: "I trust the seed. I trust the soil. I trust the promise." Every time you sow—whether it's into your church, your community, a missionary, a neighbor in need, or a friend going through something—you're not losing anything. You're setting up your future.

As we've seen, Paul said it like this:

> He who sows sparingly will also reap sparingly, and he who sows bountifully will also reap bountifully.
>
> —2 CORINTHIANS 9:6

Jesus echoed the same law when He said,

> Give, and it will be given to you: good measure, pressed down, shaken together, and running over.
>
> —LUKE 6:38

The harvest is always connected to the seed. If you want consistent increase, you need consistent sowing. It's not magic; it's the kingdom. This is how it works.

So don't just give once and wait. Don't sow for a season and then stop. Make it a way of life. Keep your hands open. Keep your heart aligned. Keep putting seed in the ground. In the kingdom of God, you can't sow without reaping, and you can't reap if you stop sowing.

To access additional resources, scan the QR code or visit thepowertoprosperbook. com/resources.

CHAPTER 27

# ENDURING PERSECUTION

**P**ROSPERITY ALWAYS PROVOKES persecution. We don't like that truth, but it's a reality we see throughout Scripture and something I've lived.

Some people argue that God never promised prosperity. Others claim that if you're being persecuted, something must be wrong with you. However, Jesus didn't say that.

As we'll see in this chapter, Jesus didn't shy away from the promise of prosperity, and He didn't shy away from the reality of persecution. He promised both.

When people message me online saying, "God doesn't promise prosperity; He promises only suffering," I tell them, "Actually, He promises both. Furthermore, one brings the other."

When you start prospering in God's favor, it provokes something in people. Not everyone celebrates your increase or cheers you on. If you don't believe me, look at Isaac's story, which we explored in chapter 7. His prosperity stirred envy among the Philistines, leading them to sabotage his wells and drive him from place to place.

You have to be prepared for that. Not everyone will understand the favor of God on your life. In fact, when you start building something with God, people will attack you the same way they did Jesus.

Persecution follows favor. Always has.

Paul talked about this tension. He experienced divine provision and said, "I have learned to be content in whatever circumstances I am" (Phil. 4:11, NASB), and "My God shall supply all your need according to His riches in glory" (Phil. 4:19). Nevertheless, he was constantly beaten, imprisoned, and persecuted. You see both: persecution and provision.

Proverbs 13:8 says, "The ransom of a man's life is his riches, but the poor does not hear rebuke." When you're prospering, you become a target. People don't sue mom-and-pop shops. They go after the big fish. Clearly, you can't separate prosperity from persecution.

But here's what you need to know: If you let persecution stop you, you won't fulfill your assignment. When Isaac's enemies filled up his wells, he didn't quit. Instead, he kept digging, moved to the next well, and dug again. Consequently, God blessed him again. That's a word for somebody—keep digging. Keep going.

When they mock you or call you greedy for preaching God's Word, remember Matthew 5:11–12:

> Blessed are you when they revile and persecute you, and say all kinds of evil against you falsely for My sake. Rejoice and be exceedingly glad, for great is your reward in heaven.

They think they're hurting you, but God says, "You're stacking up eternal rewards." If Jesus was persecuted for doing everything right, don't be surprised when it happens to you. Just make sure it's for the sake of righteousness, not foolishness.

Therefore, prospering well means enduring persecution well: standing firm, keeping your heart pure, refusing to let bitterness take root, and continuing to sow, serve, build, and obey even when it hurts.

The greater the assignment, the greater the opposition.

So if you're being persecuted for walking in God's blessing, take heart. You must be doing something right.

## The Promise of Prosperity and Persecution

People love to quote Jesus when He talks about denying yourself, taking up your cross, and following Him. That is the call: a death to the flesh and surrender of our own desires. However, what often gets overlooked is what Jesus promised immediately after. It wasn't just a message of sacrifice; it was also a message of reward.

In Mark 10:29–30 Jesus said,

> Assuredly, I say to you, there is no one who has left house or brothers or sisters or father or mother or wife or children or lands, for My sake and the gospel's, who shall not receive a hundredfold now in this time—houses and brothers and sisters and mothers and children and lands, with persecutions—and in the age to come, eternal life.

Let's pause on that. Jesus didn't say, "You'll get it all back someday, maybe." He spoke with assurance. He said *hundredfold*. And He said *now*, in this time.

Nevertheless, most believers spiritualize this verse because they're uncomfortable with how practical it is. They try to make it say something it doesn't. Jesus was explicit. He didn't just promise spiritual blessings. He listed houses, lands, and relational restoration. Then He added two words that most people skip over: *with persecutions*.

This is the pattern throughout Scripture. Prosperity and persecution walk together. You can't separate them. The same favor that causes God's blessing to rest on you will stir envy, criticism, and resistance from others. Remarkably, Jesus didn't hide this from us; He put it right there in the promise.

So if you're being blessed and being attacked, let me encourage you: You're right on track.

That's not a sign something's wrong—it's a sign something's working. It's the same pattern we see with every covenant bearer. When God's favor becomes obvious, opposition follows.

Similarly, it's the same thing Jesus experienced. His life shone with God's presence and power, and it provoked the envy and wrath of religious leaders. It triggered His crucifixion. He was sinless and perfect, yet the more He prospered in His assignment, the more opposition rose.

Don't be surprised when favor brings friction. Don't be shocked when blessing stirs up backlash. Don't water down God's promise in order to make persecution feel more palatable. Jesus never separated the two, and neither should we. He promised a hundredfold. He promised persecution. He promised eternal life.

They all come together.

## Isaac's Favor Brought Envy

Remember Isaac's journey that we explored earlier? His hundredfold harvest amid famine wasn't just a blessing; it became a target. Scripture tells us plainly: "So the Philistines envied him" (Gen. 26:14).

His blessing triggered their jealousy. His favor revealed their insecurity. Moreover, it wasn't passive resentment either. They didn't just roll their eyes at him; they actively tried to sabotage him. They filled in the wells that his father, Abraham, had dug, wells that were part of Isaac's inheritance. It's a picture of what persecution often looks like. Sometimes it's not a direct attack. Sometimes it's people trying to block your future by burying your past.

What did Isaac do? He didn't whine, retaliate, or stop. He just kept digging.

Every time a well got filled in, he moved and dug another one. Every time he dug, water came up again. Why? Because the blessing was on him. It didn't matter where he dug or who opposed him. God's favor on his life ensured that the flow would continue.

That's what happens when the covenant is real. That's what happens when your prosperity is rooted in obedience. Even when people try to cover it up, the blessing keeps rising to the surface. They can try to shut doors, but God keeps opening new ones. They can try to smear your name, but God keeps increasing your influence. They can try to block the well, but the well wasn't their source to begin with.

Isaac wasn't prospering because of favorable conditions. Rather, he was prospering because of covenant. Covenant favor doesn't stop just because people are uncomfortable with it. It multiplies in the face of resistance.

That's exactly what we're called to walk in.

## Persecution Isn't Just Personal— It's Proof of God's Favor

When you begin operating in God's blessing, don't be surprised when people misjudge your motives. Don't be shocked when people start talking behind your back or when people who used to be close suddenly grow cold or distant. It's not always because you've changed. It's because your fruit is exposing their famine.

Your breakthrough confronts their barrenness. Your increase highlights their complacency. The favor on your life becomes uncomfortable for people who have chosen to stay stagnant. If they've refused to seek God for themselves, your obedience will feel like a threat. Your harvest will feel like a rebuke. It's not because you're being prideful; it's because your results are reminding them of what's possible and what they haven't pursued.

Here's the thing: It's not your job to manage their offense. Furthermore, it's not your job to shrink back just to make them feel better or explain away the blessing so they don't feel insecure. Your job is to stay obedient, steward the blessing, walk in humility, and keep on digging.

That's exactly what Isaac did. Every time he was pushed out, every time his wells were filled up, every time he was driven from a place where he was prospering, he didn't argue, retaliate, or start a smear campaign. Instead, he moved on. Every time he moved, God blessed him again.

Eventually, the blessing became so obvious that even his enemies had to acknowledge it.

> We have certainly seen that the LORD is with you.
>
> —GENESIS 26:28

That's what happens when you persevere under pressure, when you stay the course while people try to discredit you. When you let your fruit speak louder than your critics, God will make it undeniable. The same mouths that cursed you will one day confess what they see: The Lord is with you.

## The Spirit of Mammon Will Use Persecution to Paralyze You

Let's be clear: Not all persecution comes from the world. Sometimes it comes from within the church, especially when you start prospering. That's when the religious spirit starts whispering things like, "Is this really God?" "Should they be teaching that?" "Are they just in it for the money?" It happened to Jesus, Paul, and the early church. It will happen to you.

Therefore, you have to discern where that resistance is really coming from. Often, it's not holiness speaking; it's mammon. It's that same lying spirit Jesus warned about in Matthew 6:24, the one that tries to divide your allegiance. The spirit of mammon doesn't just show up in greed. It shows up in judgment, suspicion, and false humility, and in the refusal to believe that God actually wants His people to prosper.

Mammon will have you thinking that financial blessing is something to be ashamed of, that favor is suspicious, that increase is worldly. It will twist God's Word in people's mouths and make them call the blessing evil, even when the fruit is undeniable. If the enemy can't keep you poor, he'll try to keep you afraid of becoming prosperous. He'll try to shame you for walking in what God has already said belongs to you.

He'll try to convince you that if you're prospering, you must be doing something wrong. He'll point to your generosity and call it manipulation. He'll try to make you feel guilty for the provision God sent your way. If he can't make you guilty, he'll try to make you hesitant. He'll get you second-guessing your obedience and twist your testimony into a liability.

But don't bow.

Don't let mammon's whisper stop you from testifying about what God has done. Don't apologize for the fruit growing on your tree. Jesus Himself said you would know a tree by its fruit. When the fruit starts showing up, don't shrink back because someone else is still stuck in famine. Don't retreat because someone else is uncomfortable with your harvest.

The blessing that came from covenant obedience stirred up jealousy in Isaac's time, and it will stir up jealousy in ours. His enemies didn't just envy him; they actively tried to sabotage him. They filled up the wells his father had dug and tried to bury his inheritance. Nevertheless, Isaac didn't quit, try to explain himself, or beg for their approval. He just kept digging. Every time he dug, he found water again.

That's what favor does. That's what blessing does. When God's hand is on your life, the supply keeps flowing even when people try to block it, even when they fill your wells with dirt, even when they try to cover up what God already opened. The persecution didn't stop Isaac's blessing; it just exposed it.

That's what you need to see. Persecution isn't always personal; it's often proof. Proof that God's hand is on your life. Proof that the blessing is real. Proof that you're moving forward. If you weren't advancing, the enemy wouldn't be trying to slow you down. But because you are, because the harvest is growing and the favor is obvious, mammon sends accusations, false narratives, and religious noise.

But don't bow.

Ultimately, if the blessing came from Him, don't let the backlash stop you from walking in it. Steward it with humility. Testify about it with gratitude. Keep moving forward. Because persecution isn't just proof that you're doing something right.

It's preparation for what God's about to do next.

To access additional resources, scan the QR code or visit thepowertoprosperbook.com/resources.

## CHAPTER 28

# DON'T BOW TO PHARAOH

Let's be clear about what's at stake here. This isn't just about managing your money wisely or being a good steward. This is about worship. Jesus said you can't serve two masters. You will either hate one and love the other, or you'll be loyal to one and despise the other.

> You cannot serve God and mammon.
>
> —Matthew 6:24

That's what this comes down to: two masters, two systems, two spirits. One will lead you to freedom, the other to bondage. One is the Spirit of God: your true source, your Good Shepherd, your provider. The other is mammon: a lying spirit that attaches itself to money and whispers in your ear, "You're on your own. You better figure it out. God's not going to come through this time."

We all face that temptation, regardless of how long we've been following Jesus or how much money we have. Mammon doesn't care about your bank balance; he cares only whom you serve. That's why this is such a critical line in the sand. You cannot serve both masters.

There's no middle ground. When things get tight—when business slows down, when clients cancel, when bills stack up—the true master of your heart gets revealed. Will you run to Pharaoh or wait on God? Will you bow to Pharaoh or trust Jehovah Jireh?

Someone's going to get your allegiance, and the one you serve will be the one who gets the credit.

Jesus didn't say you can't serve both God and Satan. He said you can't serve both God and mammon. Mammon is the real rival spirit because he's seductive and sneaky. He offers provision without obedience and promises security without surrender. But it's a trap.

So the question is simple: Who's your source?

If it's God, then prove it—especially when it doesn't make sense, when the numbers don't line up, when everything in your flesh says to trust the world instead. This is what it means to prosper well—not just to prosper but to prosper in a way that proves who your God really is.

## When Hardship Hits, Who Do You Run To?

God will test us in this area by allowing seasons when it doesn't seem like we're abounding. Paul said he had to learn to be content with much and with little (Phil. 4:11–12). Here's the good news: When the favor of God is with you, it doesn't matter what's going on around you. He will ensure your needs are met. You'll be like a fruitful tree bearing fruit in every season (Ps. 1:3). That's a promise from the Word of God if you are connected to Him.

However, God will allow seasons that look like lack, when things appear to be diminishing. Why? To test your allegiance.

Remember the Israelites who were delivered from Egypt after four hundred years of slavery. As we've seen, they built Pharaoh's empire while being fed daily, but they were treated harshly. God liberated them through Moses, brought them through the wilderness, and led them toward a land flowing with milk and honey. They were on their way to prosperity, but in the in-between they became discontent. Even though God fed them every day with manna from heaven, quail on the ground, and water from a rock, they started looking back and romanticizing Egypt. "It was better in Egypt," they said.

This is what happens during tough seasons. We start entertaining the idea of going back to Pharaoh, back to man, back to worldly systems, back to Egypt. But God has a different plan.

When Isaac faced famine, the Lord didn't send him to seek help from worldly powers. Instead, God said, "Stay where I told you to stay. Do what I told you to do." Isaac chose obedience over what looked like obvious provision elsewhere, and that was the key to his breakthrough.

God will test your allegiance the same way. When things feel scarce, when the bank account is tight, when clients dry up, when there's pressure on all sides, who do you run to? Do you go to a wealthy family member? Do you seek government assistance? Or do you go to God?

The test isn't about provision; it's about direction. It's about who you trust when things get tough. Will you remember the Lord your God, or will you start scrambling for other sources?

God is asking, "Will you trust Me in the famine? Will you obey Me when it doesn't make sense? Will you stay planted when everything in you wants to run?"

If you do, He'll prosper you right there where it looks dry and barren. He'll make water come out of the ground. But you have to trust Him, not the system, not Pharaoh, not Egypt, not man. Him.

## Egypt Looks Safer, but It's a Setup

God made it clear to Isaac, and He's making it clear to us: "If you stay where I've called you, even when it doesn't make sense, I'll bless you there." He didn't say to wait for the economy to bounce back or for the famine to lift. He said, "Dwell in this land…and I will perform the oath which I swore to Abraham your father" (Gen. 26:3). The blessing isn't dependent on your environment; it's dependent on your obedience.

Some people may argue, "Well, Kap, that's easy for you to say. You live in America. You have access to things others don't." But this blessing didn't originate in America. It was first spoken thousands of years ago to a man named Isaac on the other side of the planet. The reason he prospered wasn't because of his geography but because of his obedience.

The challenge for us remains: Will we obey even when Egypt looks easier? Will we follow God when the wilderness feels more uncertain? Will we stay planted where He tells us to stay even when we don't see immediate results?

God is testing your allegiance, and Egypt is the test. Egypt always looks appealing when you're under pressure, but it's a setup. If you go back to Egypt, you're trusting in chariots instead of trusting in God. When you trust in Egypt, you forfeit the very inheritance God has for you.

So what's it going to be? Obedience in famine or comfort in compromise? One leads to covenant fulfillment; the other keeps you enslaved. You can't do both.

Stay in the land God gave you. Plant your seed. Trust His promise. He will bless you there.

## The Antichrist Wants to Be Your Provider

This is one of the most important revelations God's ever shown me, and I don't hear many people talking about it.

If you and I don't make the decision now to trust God as our provider, we are unknowingly making an allegiance with what the apostle John called the "spirit of the Antichrist" (1 John 4:3). When the time of pressure comes—and it's already starting to build—if we're not anchored in God as our source, we're going to get swept away.

When the real Antichrist rises up, he will demand global allegiance. He will cause everyone—small and great, rich and poor—to receive a mark (Rev. 13:16), and without that mark you won't be able to buy or sell.

Think about that. You won't be able to participate in the economy unless you bow to his system. If we haven't trained ourselves to rely on God as our provider now, if we're still running to Pharaoh for help when things get tight, what makes us think we'll stand strong when the Antichrist offers us comfort and convenience in exchange for our worship?

The parallel is undeniable. The mark of the beast isn't just about commerce; it's about allegiance, provision, and a direct mockery of what God already established in Deuteronomy 6. God told His people to bind His Word on their hands and between their eyes. God was essentially saying, "I want My law, My covenant, to govern how you think and how you live. I want My promises to be what drive your decisions and direct your work."

Then the Antichrist comes along and mimics it. Why? Because he's a thief and a counterfeiter. He doesn't create anything original; he just corrupts what God made. When you see this mark being required on the hand and forehead, it's not just about economic regulation. It's about worship, authority, and who you trust to take care of you.

That's why Deuteronomy 8:18 is such a critical verse to repeat in this conversation:

> And you shall remember the LORD your God, for it is He who gives
> you power to get wealth, that He may establish His covenant which
> He swore to your fathers, as it is this day.

This verse isn't just about increase; it's also about allegiance. It's about God proving through your prosperity that He is who He says He is—a covenant-keeping God. If we forget that, we open the door to the counterfeit and end up giving credit to systems and structures that have no power to save.

For me, I've made a decision. I'm not going to Pharaoh for provision. I'm not putting my trust in Egypt. I'm not depending on a paycheck from a king who doesn't know my name. I'm depending on God and remembering the Lord my God, not just for what He's done in the past but for what He's promised to do now.

Jesus is my source. Not man, not culture, not the government, not an algorithm. Him.

He doesn't need the world's system to prosper me. He is the system. He is the source. He's the only One who gets the glory for every blessing in my life.

## Prosper Where God Plants You

What God told Isaac in Genesis 26 is the same thing He's saying to us today: "Don't go down to Egypt. Stay where I tell you to stay." When the land looked dry and resources were scarce, Egypt looked like the smart move—that's where the money and comfort were, where the world said to go. But God said, "Stay." And Isaac obeyed.

He simply sowed where God planted him. As we've seen, the Bible says he reaped a hundredfold in the same year. He didn't just survive; he prospered because the Lord blessed him. That's what happens when you trust God instead of bowing to Pharaoh.

This isn't about what economy you live in, whether your government is stable, or whether your inflation rate is low. It's not about where your job is or who the president is. Isaac prospered in the middle of a famine not because the land was good but because God was with him. That's the power of covenant and obedience. The favor of God is not limited by what's happening in the natural. When you stay planted in the land God called you to, even if it doesn't make sense, He will cause supernatural increase to come to you.

Too many believers are running to Egypt—back to Pharaoh, to man, to government assistance, to kings and rulers and systems of this world—when what God is really asking is, "Do you trust Me to be your source?" If you're always looking to man, to the market, to the world's systems for your provision, that's not faith. That's fear. Fear will always take you back to slavery.

Let's stop asking what looks better and start asking what God said. Provision isn't found in what looks right; it's found where He told you to stay. That's where the blessing is. That's where the power to get wealth will be released. That's where He performs His promise—not in Egypt but in obedience.

So don't bow to Pharaoh. Don't run back to Pharaoh. Don't compromise to survive. You serve a different King. When you obey His voice—even in famine, even when it looks foolish, even when others are leaving—you'll see Him do what only He can do.

He'll bless you. He'll multiply you. He'll prove to everyone around you that He is with you.

Just like He did with Isaac.

To access additional resources, scan the QR code or visit thepowertoprosperbook.com/resources.

## CHAPTER 29

# FINAL CHARGE AND COMMISSION

I F YOU'VE MADE it this far in the book, you're not the same person who started. You may have opened this with hesitation, theological questions, or past wounds from how you've seen prosperity misused. Perhaps you were simply trying to get clarity on how to honor God with your money without compromising your convictions. But you've now seen the Word for yourself. You've heard what God actually says and been shown the covenant, not the counterfeit.

You've been taken on a journey—from breaking the religious mindset around money to understanding the laws that govern prosperity to being equipped to prosper well in a way that honors God and leaves a legacy. The time has come to decide what you're going to do.

This can't be just another Christian book you read, highlight, and put on a shelf. This needs to become a turning point: a before-and-after moment, a marker in your story where you stop wondering whether God wants to bless you and start living like He already has. This is where you stop trying to build safety and start building something that outlives you. This is where you decide that money will never be your master again. You're not called to survive. You're called to advance, to multiply, to fund what matters most to God.

Everything in this book has pointed to one truth: Prosperity is not the end goal—obedience is. When you obey God, remember Him as your source, steward what He puts in your hands, and sow what's in His heart, prosperity becomes the by-product. Provision follows purpose. It always has. It always will.

He never promised that you wouldn't face resistance. But He did promise that if you trust Him, follow His laws, and live for His glory, He will bless the work of your hands.

As you turn this final page, I want to leave you with the verse that launched this entire journey: "Remember the LORD your God, for it is He who gives you power to get wealth, that He may establish His covenant which He swore to your fathers, as it is this day" (Deut. 8:18).

That's not hype. That's not theory. That's a covenant promise.

He gives you power—not to chase money but to confirm His covenant. He prospers you—not to impress others but to build something eternal. Your responsibility now is to remember Him in everything you do.

Remember Him when you budget and when you sow. Remember Him when you're tempted to cling tightly and when He opens doors and multiplies what's in your hand. Remember Him when He elevates you and when others misunderstand you. Remember Him when your barns are filled and your vats are overflowing. Always remember that it is He who gave you the power to get wealth.

You've been entrusted with this message. The time has come to live it.

The world doesn't need more people who talk about money. It needs more people who manage it like it belongs to God. The church doesn't need more sermons on generosity. It needs more examples of legacy builders who refuse to bow to mammon and who carry the weight of eternal impact with joy and conviction.

You are that person. This is your moment. Go build what outlives you.

You have God's permission, and power, to prosper.

## Final Declaration

If you're ready to step into this, speak this out loud:

*Thank You, Father, that I am called to prosper.*
*You want to trust me with wealth.*
*And by Your power, I will steward it well.*
*I will not bow to fear, culture, or compromise.*
*I will multiply what You have placed in my hands.*
*I will build a legacy that outlives me.*
*And I will remember You, the Lord my God, always.*
*This is the charge.*
*This is Your covenant with me.*
*This is my commission.*
*I receive it in full today.*
*In Jesus' name, amen.*

# A PERSONAL INVITATION
# FROM THE AUTHOR

**G**OD LOVES YOU deeply. His Word is filled with promises that reveal His desire to bring healing, hope, and abundant life to every area of your being: body, mind, and spirit. More than anything, He wants a personal relationship with you through His Son, Jesus Christ.

If you've never invited Jesus into your life, you can do so right now. It's not about religion; it's about a relationship with the One who knows you completely and loves you unconditionally. If you're ready to take that step, simply pray this prayer with a sincere heart:

> *Lord Jesus, I want to know You as my Savior and Lord. I confess and believe that You are the Son of God and that You died for my sins. I believe that You rose from the dead and are alive today. Please forgive me for my sins. I invite You into my heart and my life. Make me new. Help me walk with You, grow in Your love, and live for You every day. In Jesus' name, amen.*

If you just prayed that prayer, you've made the most important decision of your life. All of heaven rejoices with you, and so do I! You are now a child of God, and your journey with Him has just begun.

To hear me personally share about what it means to follow Christ, scan the QR code or visit thepowertoprosperbook.com/resources.

Please reach out to my publisher at pray4me@charismamedia.com if you accepted Jesus today or if this book has encouraged or impacted your life in any way. We'd love to celebrate with you and send you free materials to help strengthen your faith. We look forward to hearing from you!

# NOTES

## CHAPTER 2

1.  "How Income Varies Among US Religious Groups," Pew Research Center, October 11, 2016, https://www.pewresearch.org/short-reads/2016/10/11/how-income-varies-among-u-s-religious-groups/.
2.  "38% of US Pastors Have Thought About Quitting Full-Time Ministry in the Past Year," Barna, November 16, 2021, https://www.barna.com/research/pastors-well-being/.
3.  "Evangelical Pastor Study" for National Association of Evangelicals, Grey Matter Research, July 2015, https://greymatterresearch.com/wp-content/uploads/2019/07/NAE-Grey-Matter-Pastor-Study-Report_July-2015.pdf.
4.  "Critical Issues in North American Church Planting: #1 Money," jdpayne.org, February 27, 2010, https://www.jdpayne.org/2010/02/critical-issues-in-north-american-church-planting-1-money/.
5.  David Roach, "In Church Planting, More Money Means More People," *Christianity Today*, February 2023, https://www.christianitytoday.com/2023/01/church-planting-costs-startup-money-metrics/.

## CHAPTER 9

1.  "History: Christ Is for All Nations," Christ for All Nations, accessed August 28, 2025, https://cfan.org/history; James O. Davis, "Ten Life Lessons from Evangelist Reinhard Bonnke's Life and Ministry," Global Church Network, December 10, 2019, https://gcnw.tv/2019/12/10/ten-life-lessons-from-evangelist-reinhard-bonnkes-life-ministry/.

## CHAPTER 14

1.  "Thomas A. Edison Quotes," BrainyQuote, accessed August 4, 2025, https://www.brainyquote.com/quotes/thomas_a_edison_132683.

## CHAPTER 24

1.  "A List of Bible Verses on Poverty, Justice, and Compassion," Sojourners, accessed August 26, 2025, https://sojo.net/list-some-more-2000verses-scripture-poverty-and-justice.

# ABOUT THE AUTHOR

Kap Chatfield is a Christian content creator, filmmaker, pastor, speaker, and coach who has directed two feature-length documentaries, *Acts* and *The Time Is Now*. His social media presence serves millions of people online every month. He is a teaching pastor at Love Church in Omaha, Nebraska. He and his wife, Joy, have four children.

kapchatfield.com